I0390697

A Photographic Tribute To
Mistress Benay

A Pictorial Look At The Life Of A Preeminent Dominatrix and Author

By

Her Loving Husband Slave Troy

©DSC Publishing 2019

A Photographic Tribute To
Mistress Benay

A Pictorial Look At The Life Of A Preeminent Dominatrix and Author

By

Her Loving Husband Slave Troy

__Author's Note:__ This Pictorial Novel is intended strictly for adult readers. If you are under the age of eighteen, or are offended by Depictions of Sexual Activity, Female Domination, Female Led Relationships, Male Chastity, Bisexuality, or BDSM related topics, please continue no further since this Novel may graphically depict such sexual activities.

No one Reading this Novel or Viewing the Pictures contained within should ever undertake any of the actions portrayed in this book without taking the appropriate safety precautions, as well as obtaining the mutual consent of their partner/partners, before engaging in such activity.

All materials, including Pictures and Text contained herein are the sole property of the Author and DSC Publishing, and may not be reproduced or used in any manner or means mechanical or electronic without the express written permission and consent of the author and the Publishing Company.

Table of Contents

A Complete List of Exciting Books Published on Amazon by Mistress Benay Over the Years is Presented Here for Your Benefit:

You can visit Mistress Benay's Author's Page on Amazon to view her Bio and see in-depth information about all of her Books.

This Book is Dedicated to my Dear Wife Benay who left this Earth at such a Young Age and took half of my Heart with Her

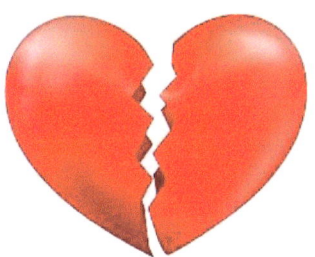

"Life Is Not Measured By The Breaths We Take

But By The Moments Which Take Our Breath Away"

This was the Motto by Which my Dear Wife and Sweetheart Benay lived Her Life!

Mistress Benay September,1953 – March, 2018

Rest In Peace

I Miss You Terribly, Cry for You Each Day, and I Long to See Your Lovely Smiling Face and Hear your Beautiful Voice Once Again

… Your Loving Husband

July 2019

Mistress Benay In Her Dungeon

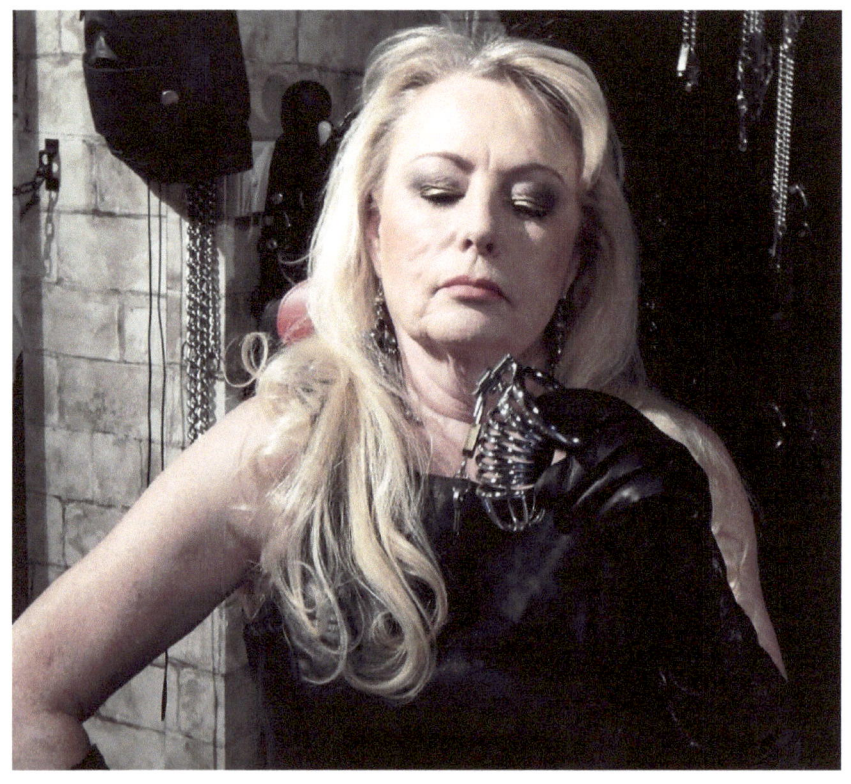

The Mistress was contemplating Locking Up Another Slave

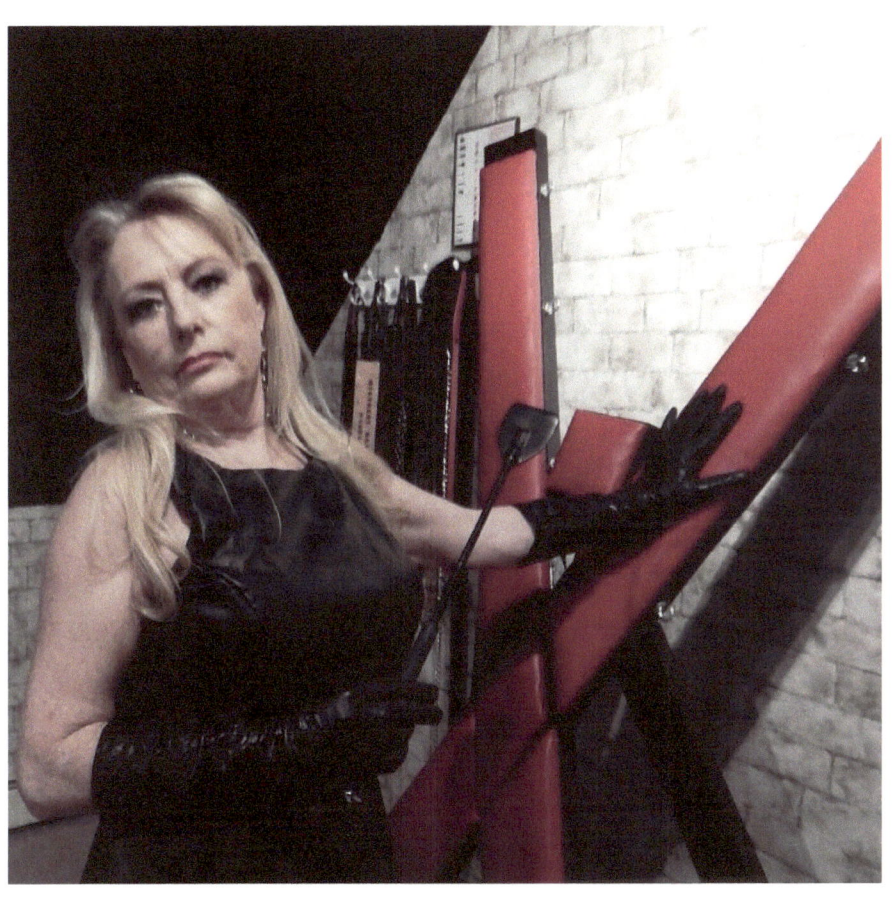

Countless "Victims" were Restrained Helplessly to The Cross in Mistress Benay's Dungeon

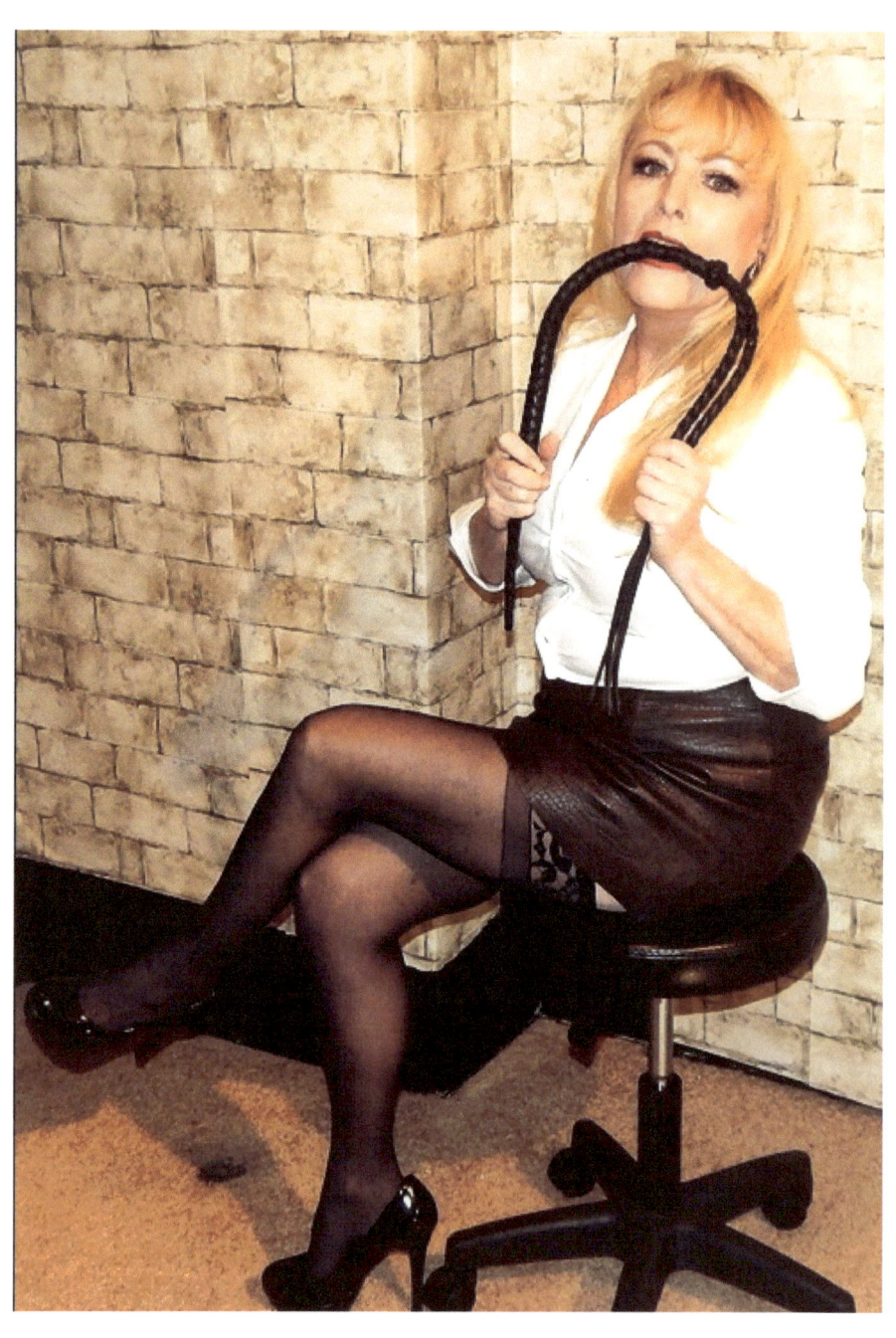

Many a slave felt the Sting of Mistress Benay's Whip when visiting her Dungeon!

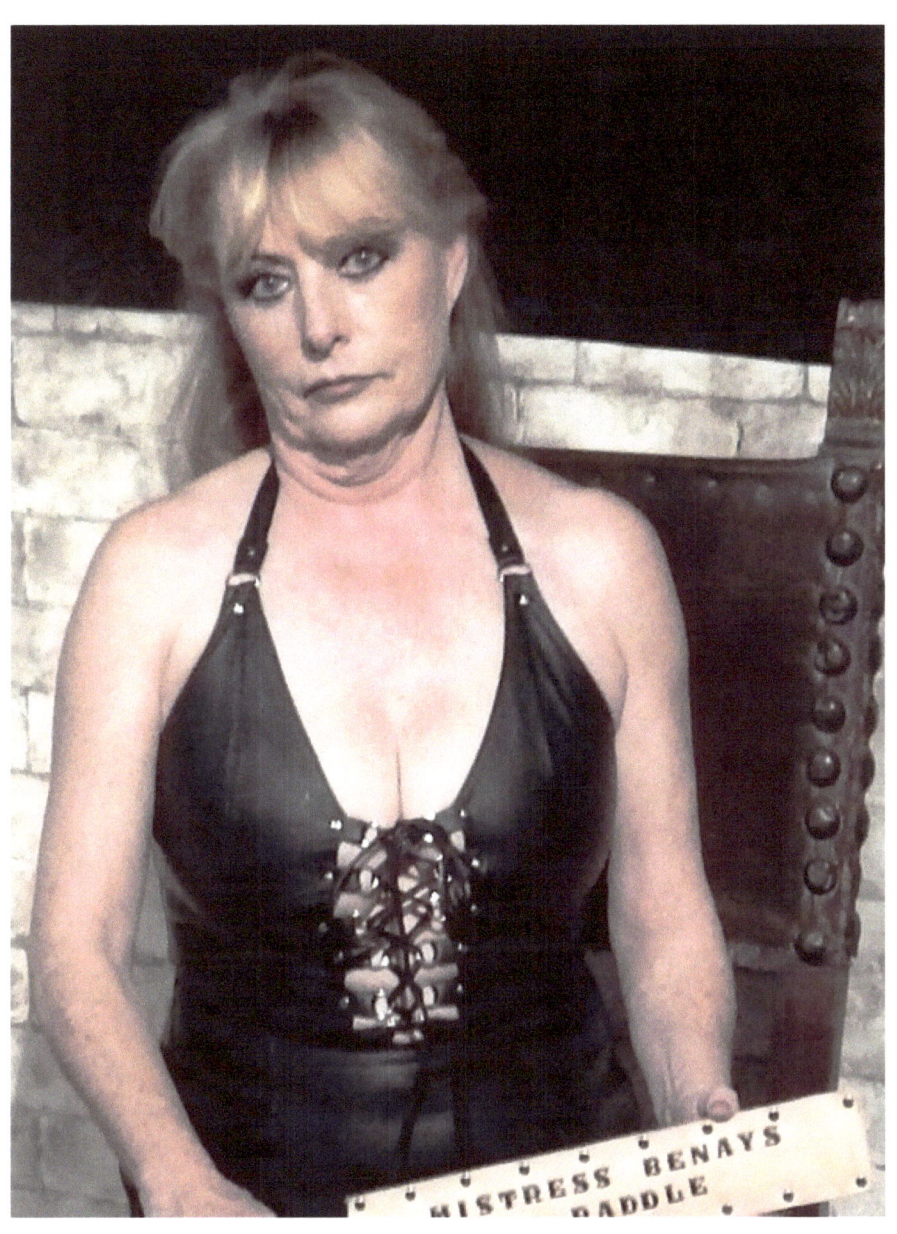

If you were ever punished by Mistress Benay's Special Paddle, you'll remember it for the rest of your life!

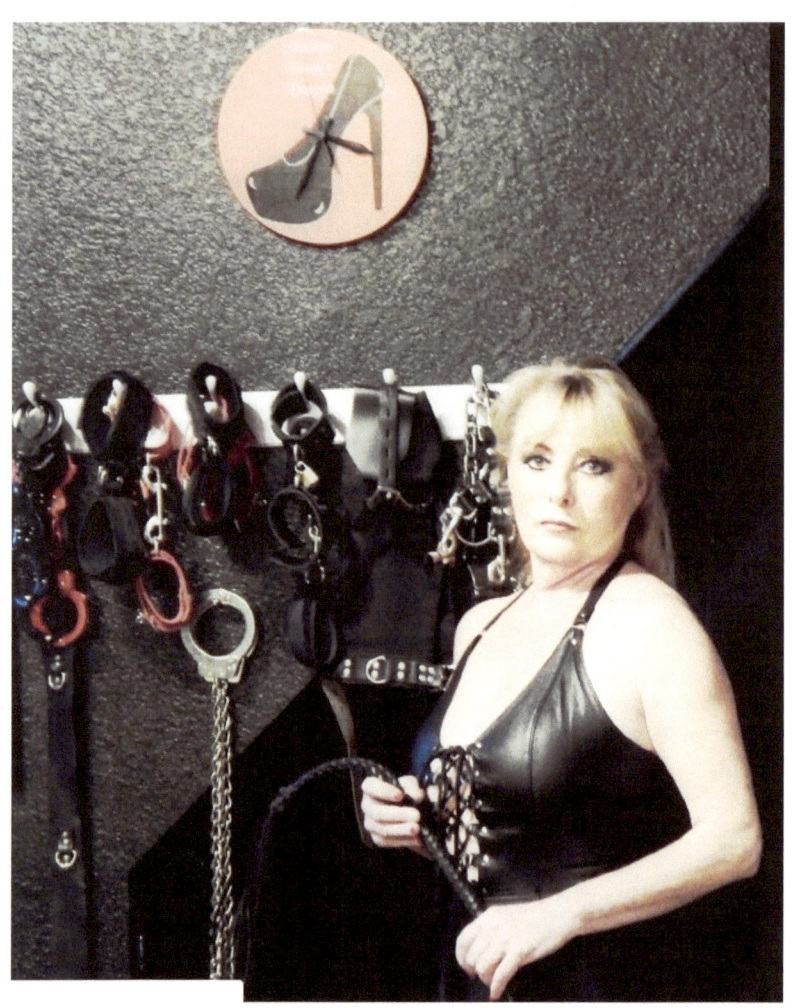

The Mistress's Dungeon had Every type of Possible Restraint to keep a slave helpless!

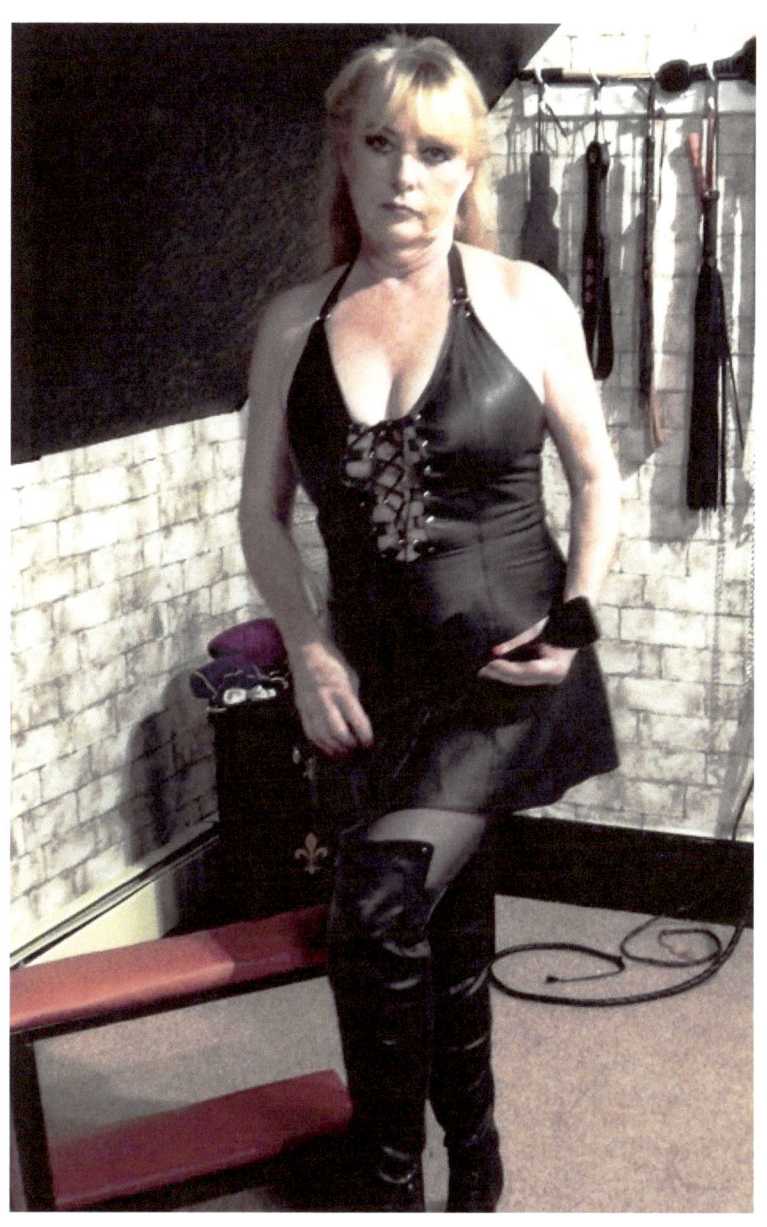

So Many Wonderful Implements of Punishment in
Mistress Benay's Dungeon

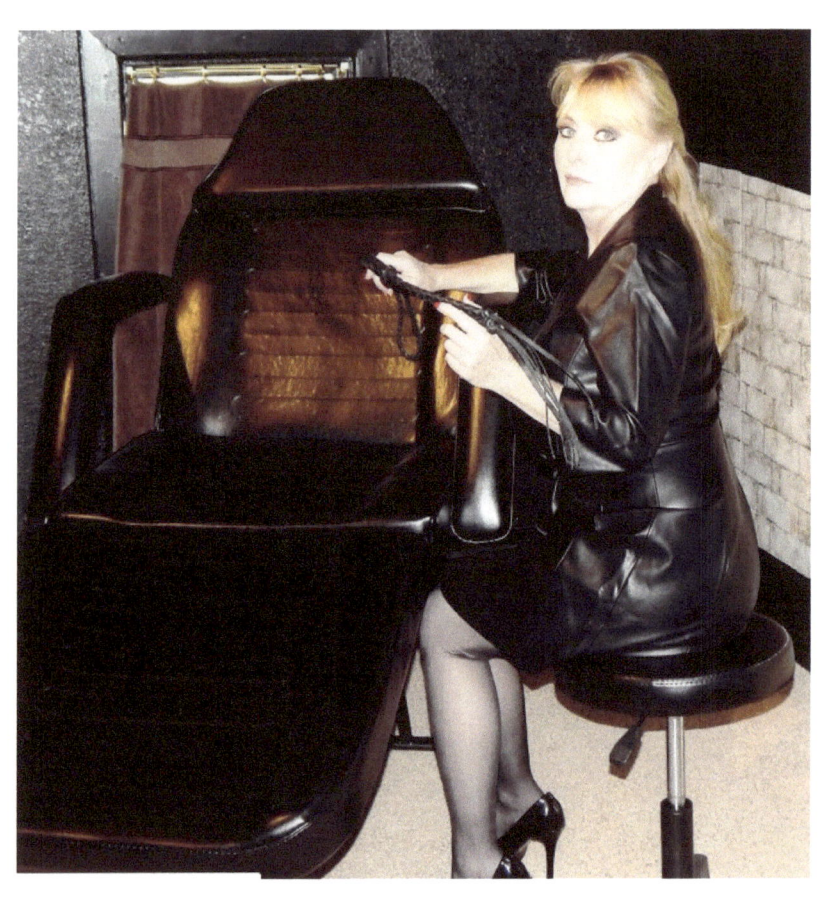

The Special Chair which Mistress Benay used to Interrogate Victims

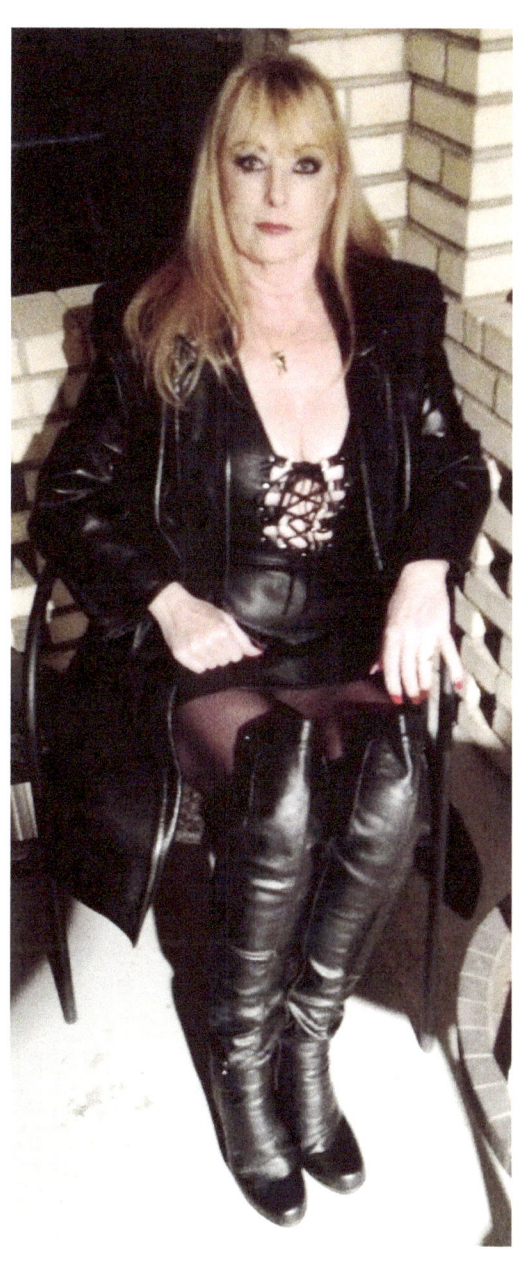

Mistress Benay waiting for a chastity slave to arrive at the Pueblo Dungeon

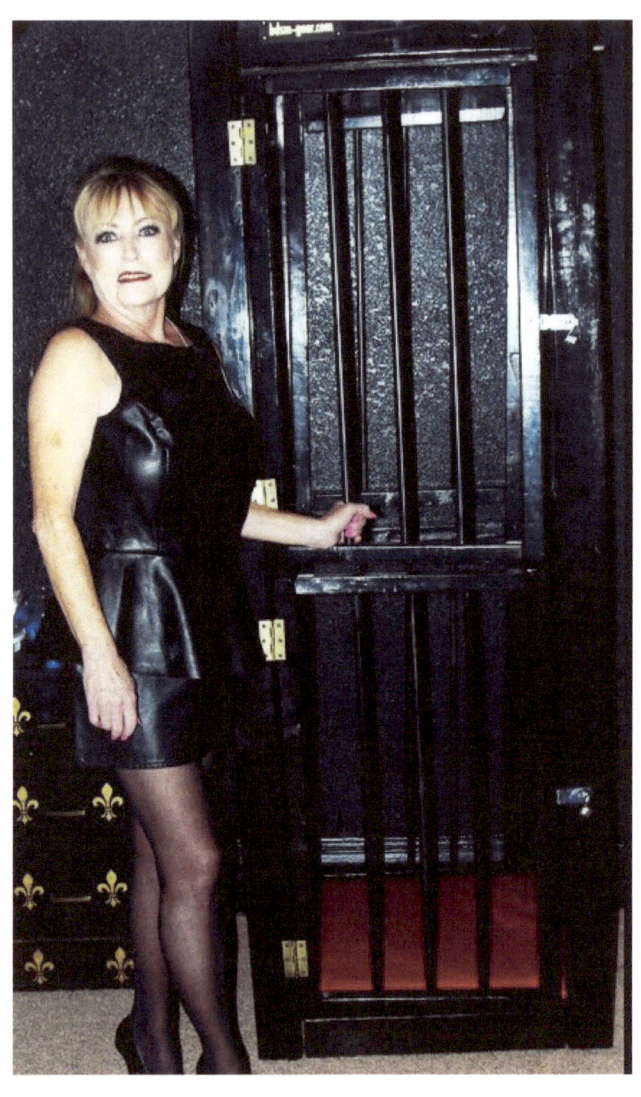

Only The Mistress Knew how long a slave would stay Locked in Her Vertical Cage!

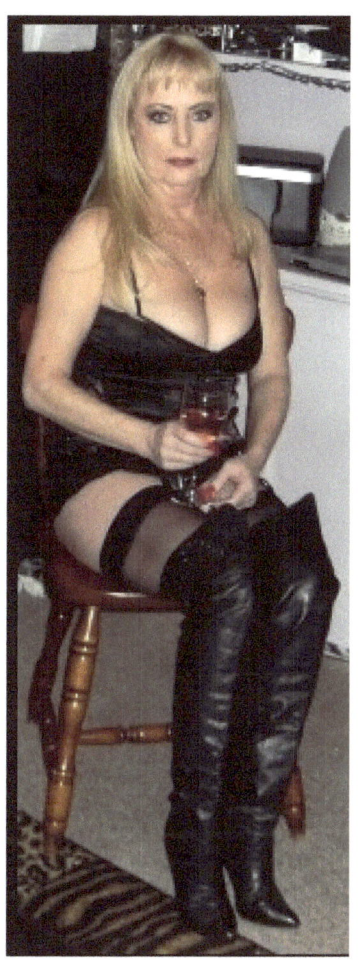

All slaves were always required to Worship The Mistress's Boots immediately upon entering Her Dungeon!

Mistress Benay at the 1763 Atlanta Dungeon

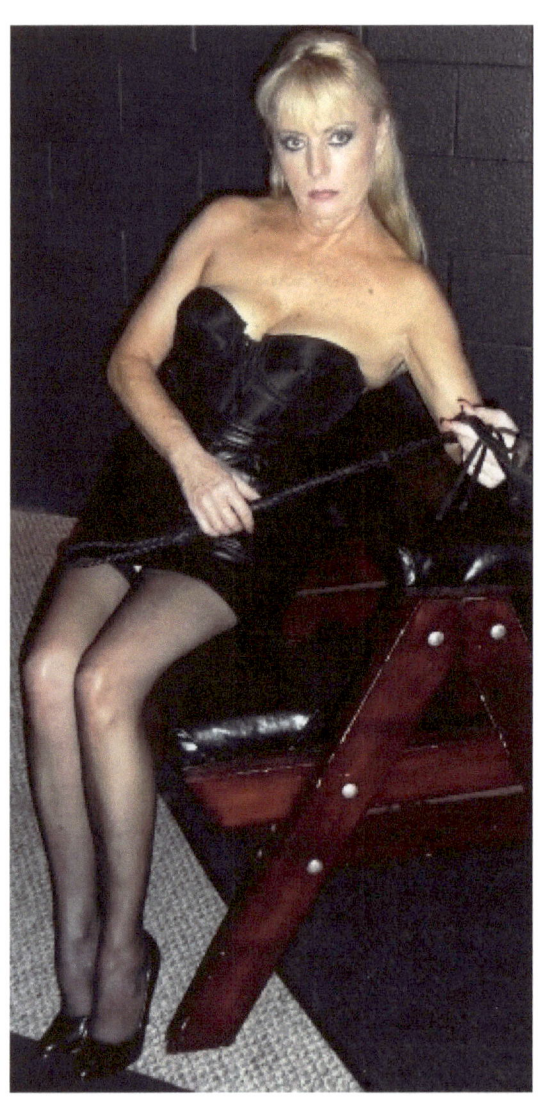

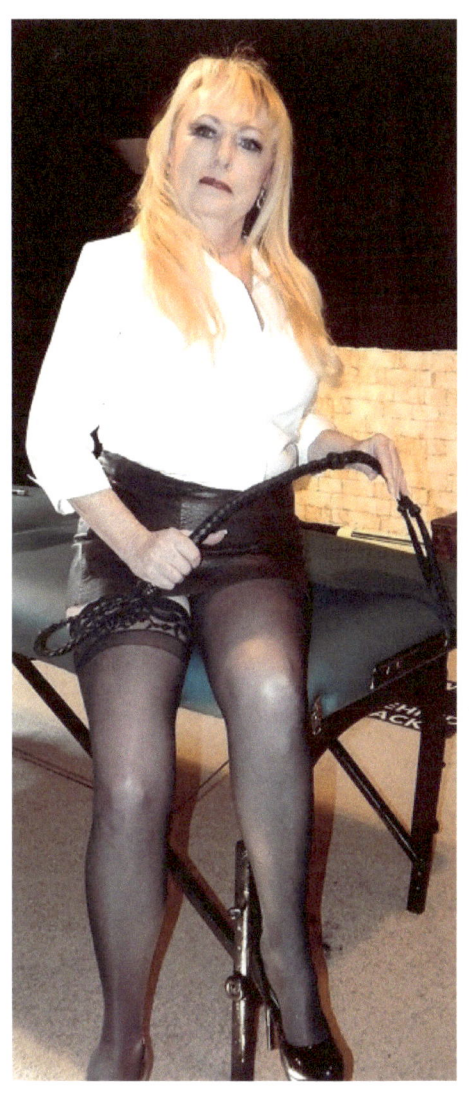

If you were fortunate enough to have had a Session with Mistress Benay in her Dungeon, I know that you'll cherish that Memory Forever!

Mistress Benay At Play With Her Slave

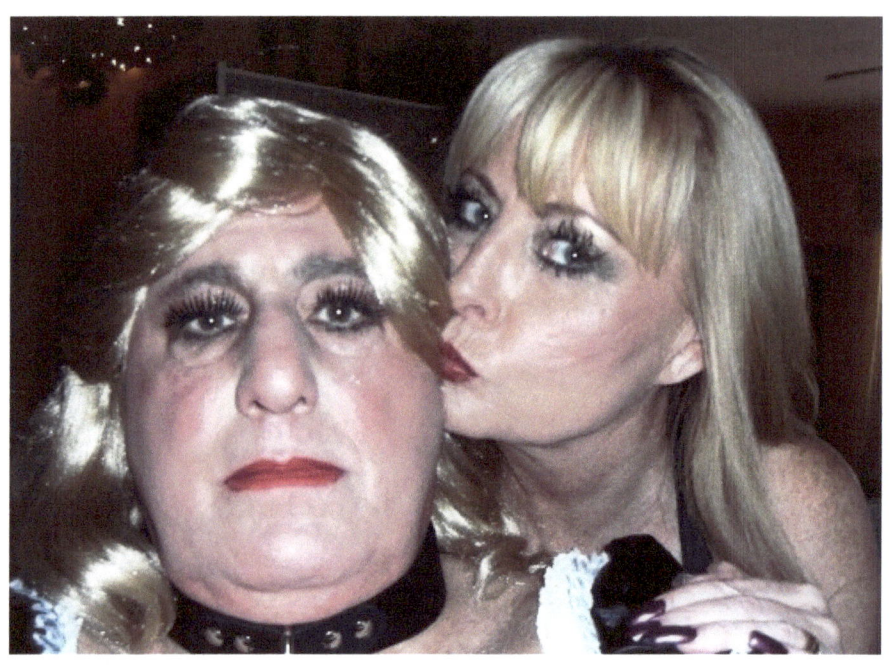

The Mistress Loved Dressing Troy up as Her Sissy Slave Trina

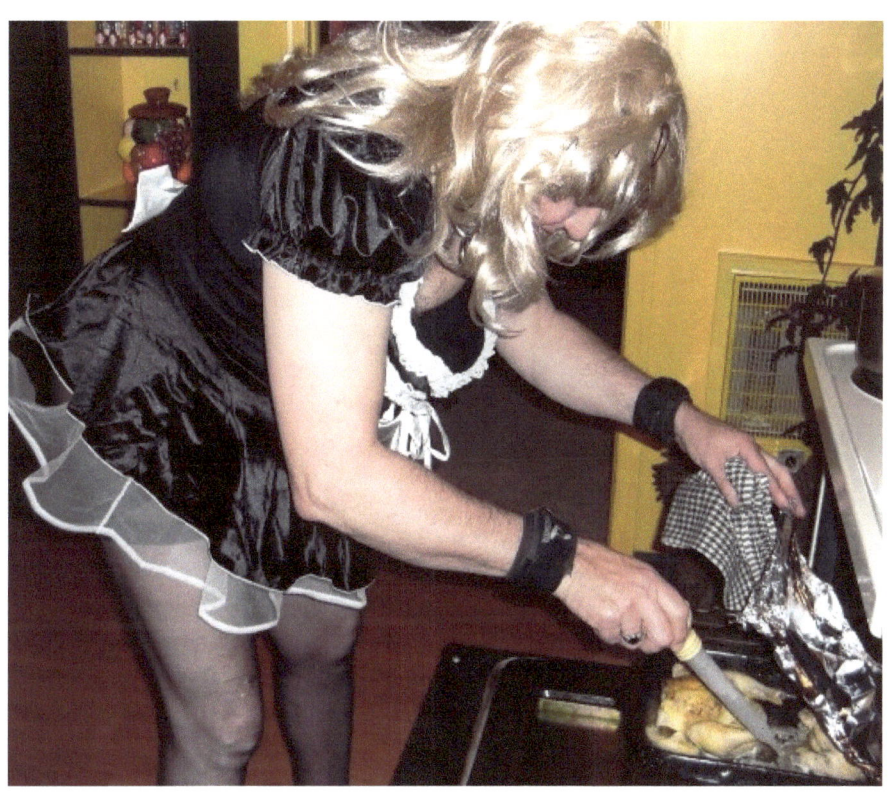

*Sissy slave **Trina** preparing Dinner for Mistress Benay*

The Mistress is obviously upset with her slave for some reason!

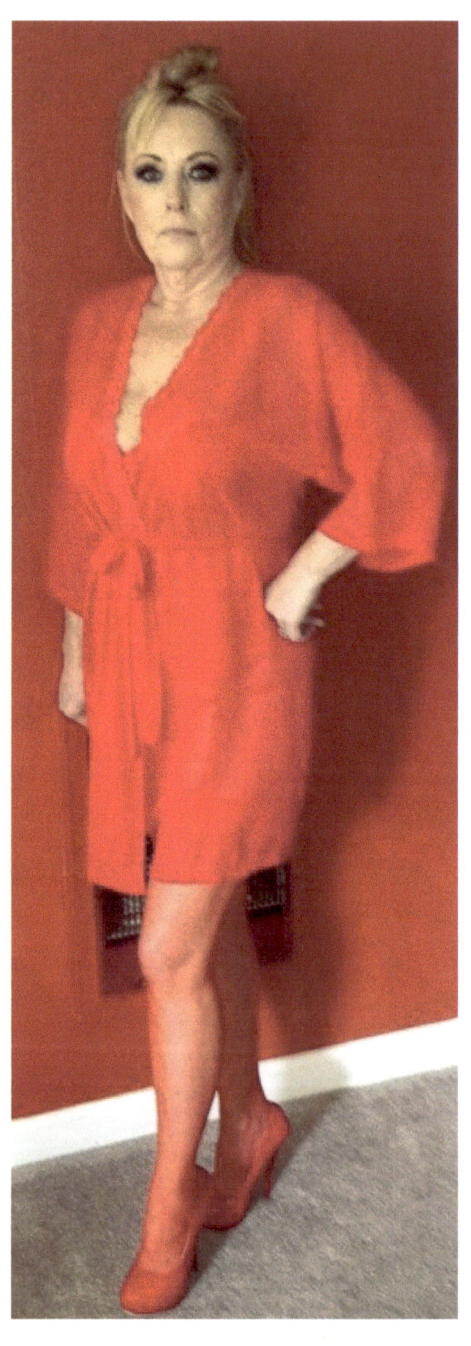

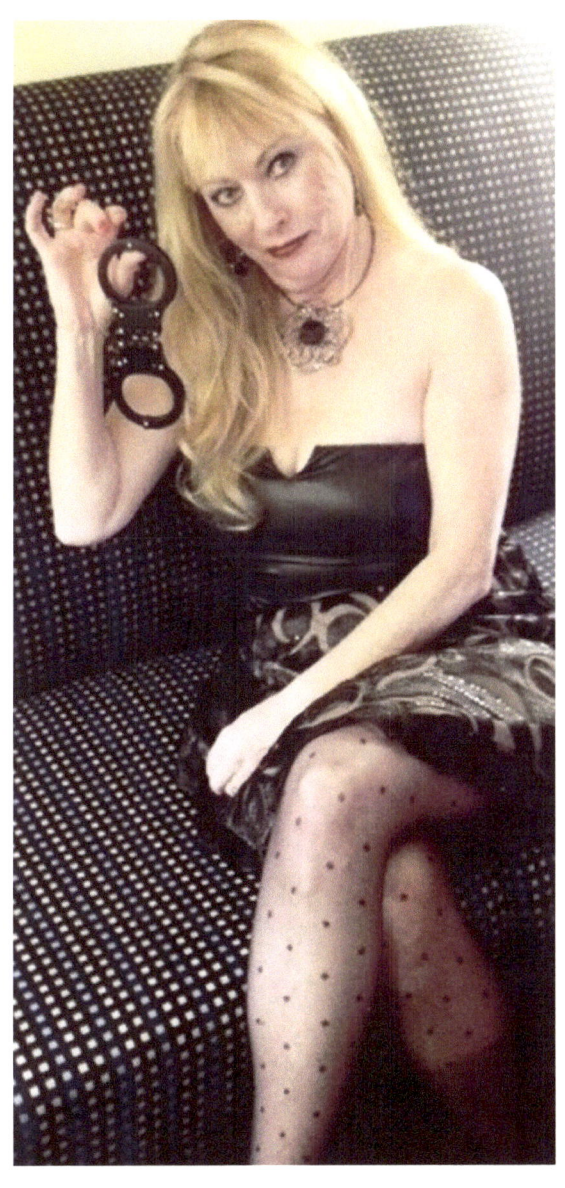

Once those Cuffs were Locked onto Troy's Wrists, he was truly at the Mercy of Mistress Benay!

Troy was on his best behavior this night, and did everything in his power to please his Mistress

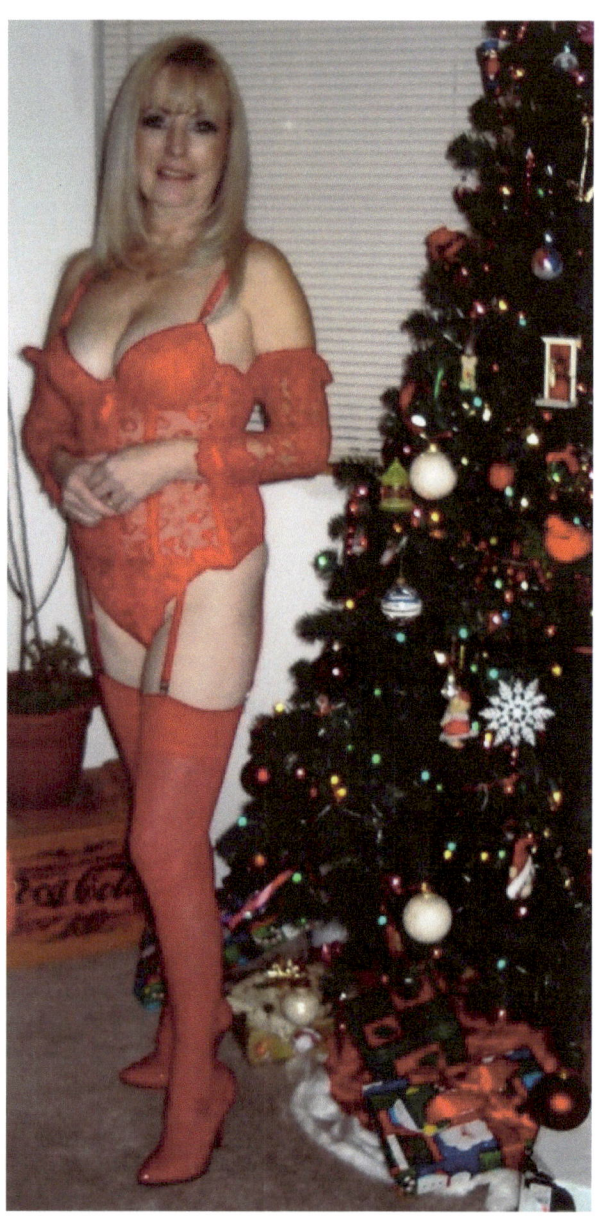

Mistress Benay Loved to Dress Up and Role Play

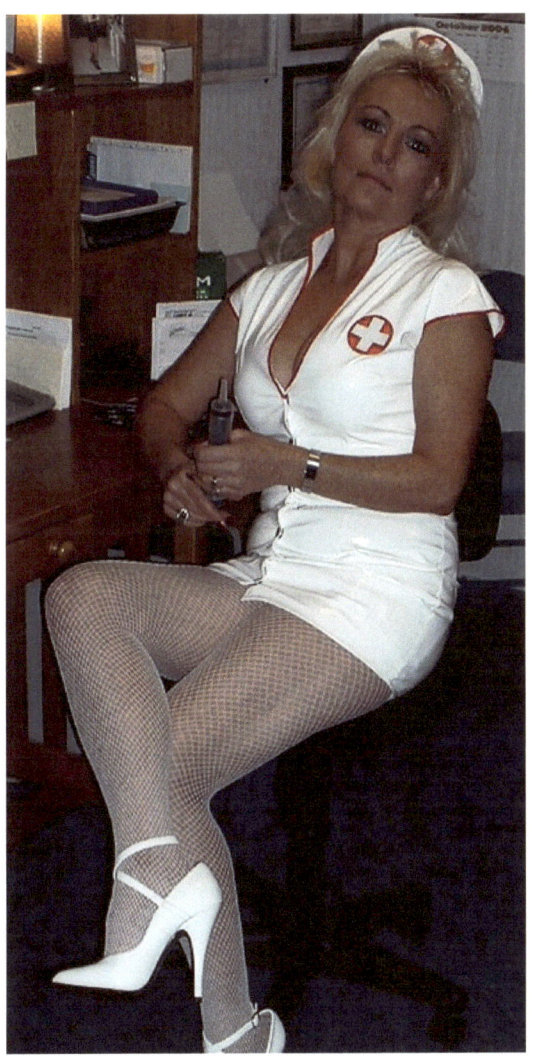

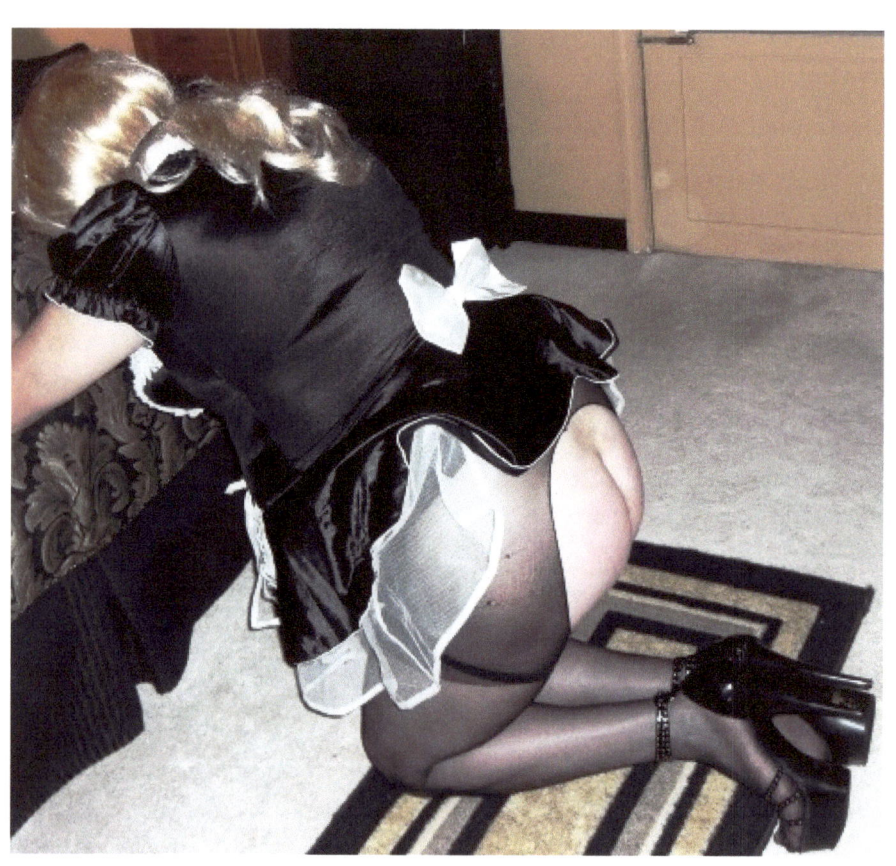

Sissy slave Trina had to assume the position to await her Punishment for Disappointing Mistress Benay

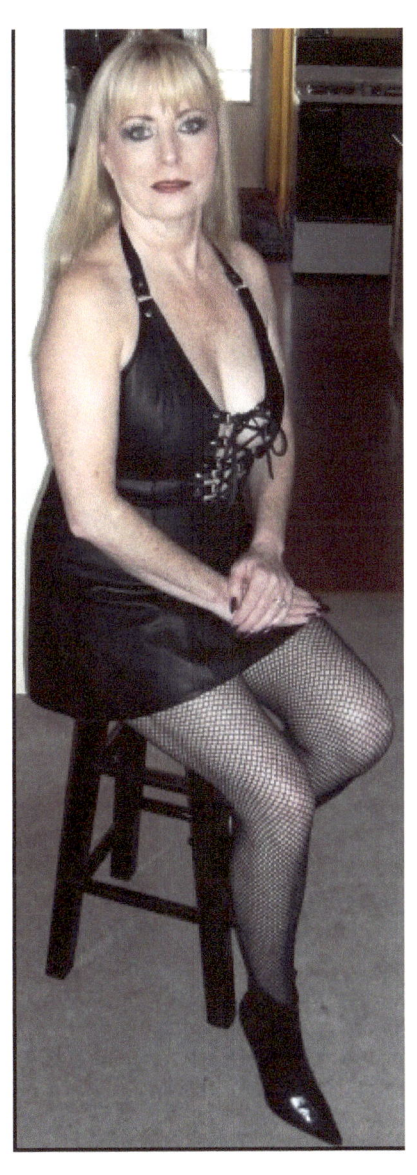

The Mistress Waits as Her slave crawls to Her on his hands and knees!

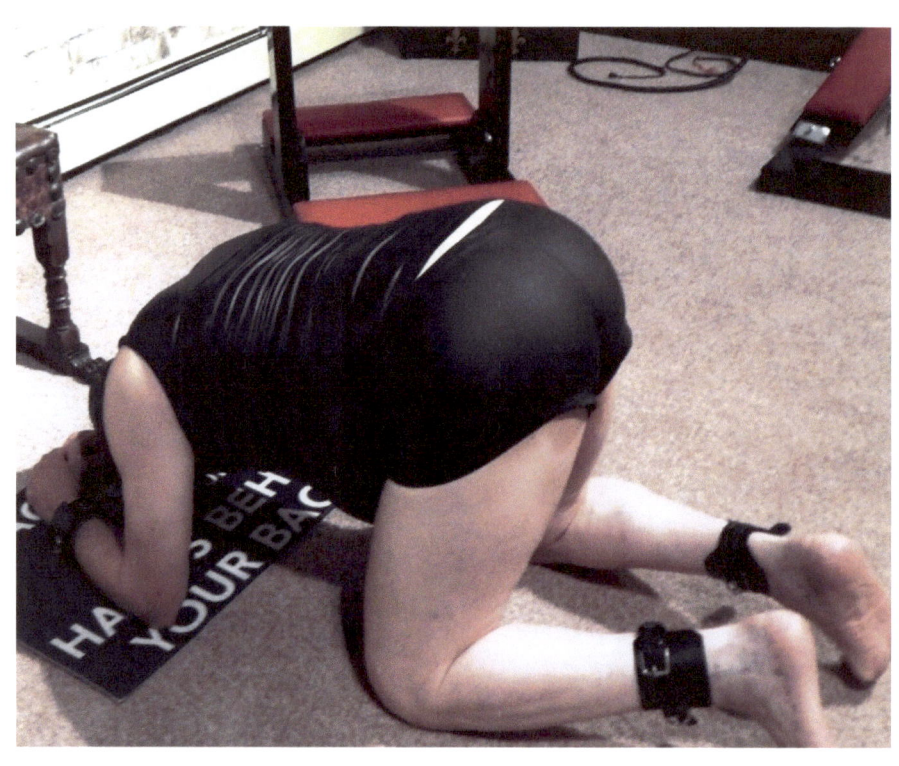

This slave has no idea as to what Punishment awaits him once Mistress Benay enters her Dungeon!

Mistress Benay At Work In Her Office & On The Road

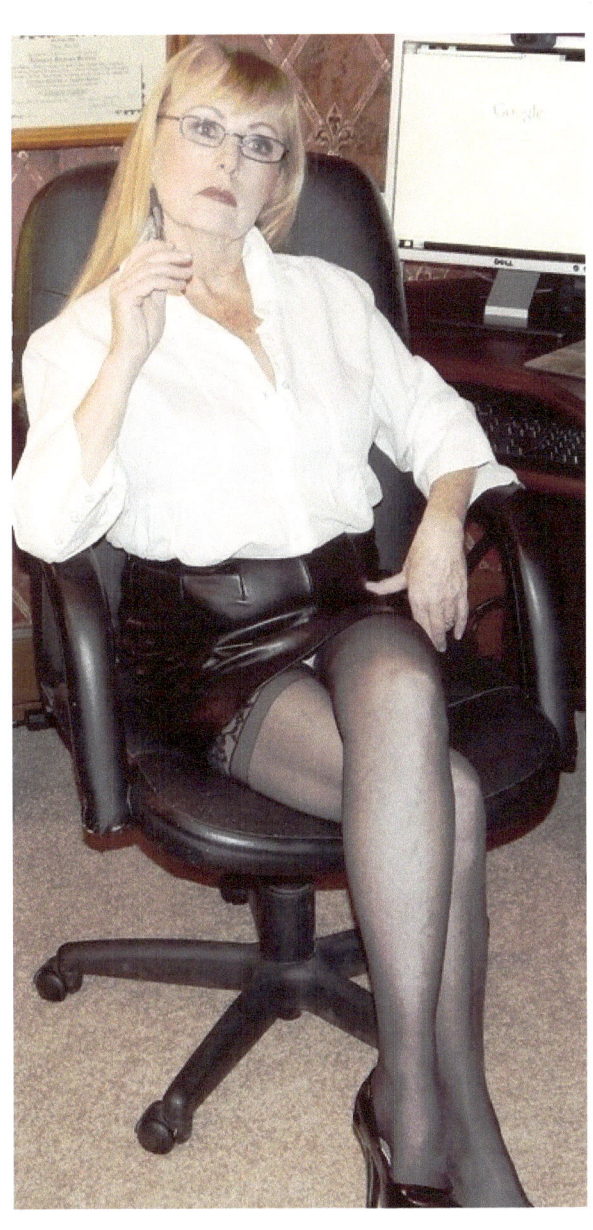

Mistress Benay at the "Thunder In The Mountains"
Fetish Convention in Denver

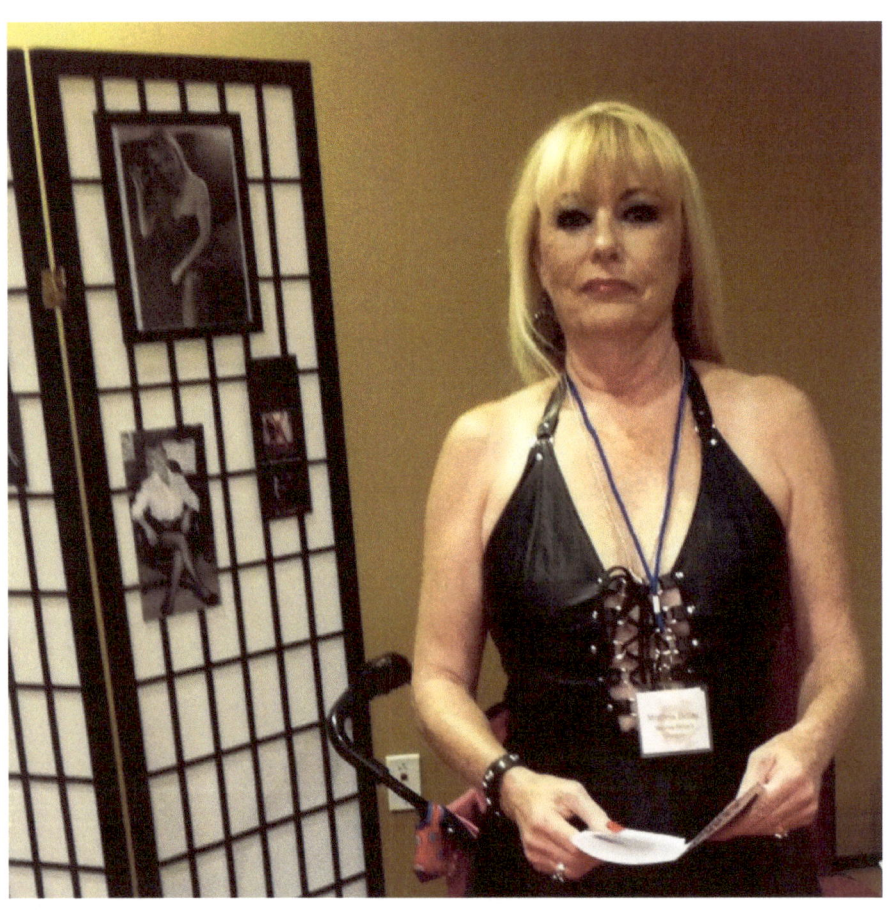

The Mistress gathering her thoughts before starting another Sensuous Novel

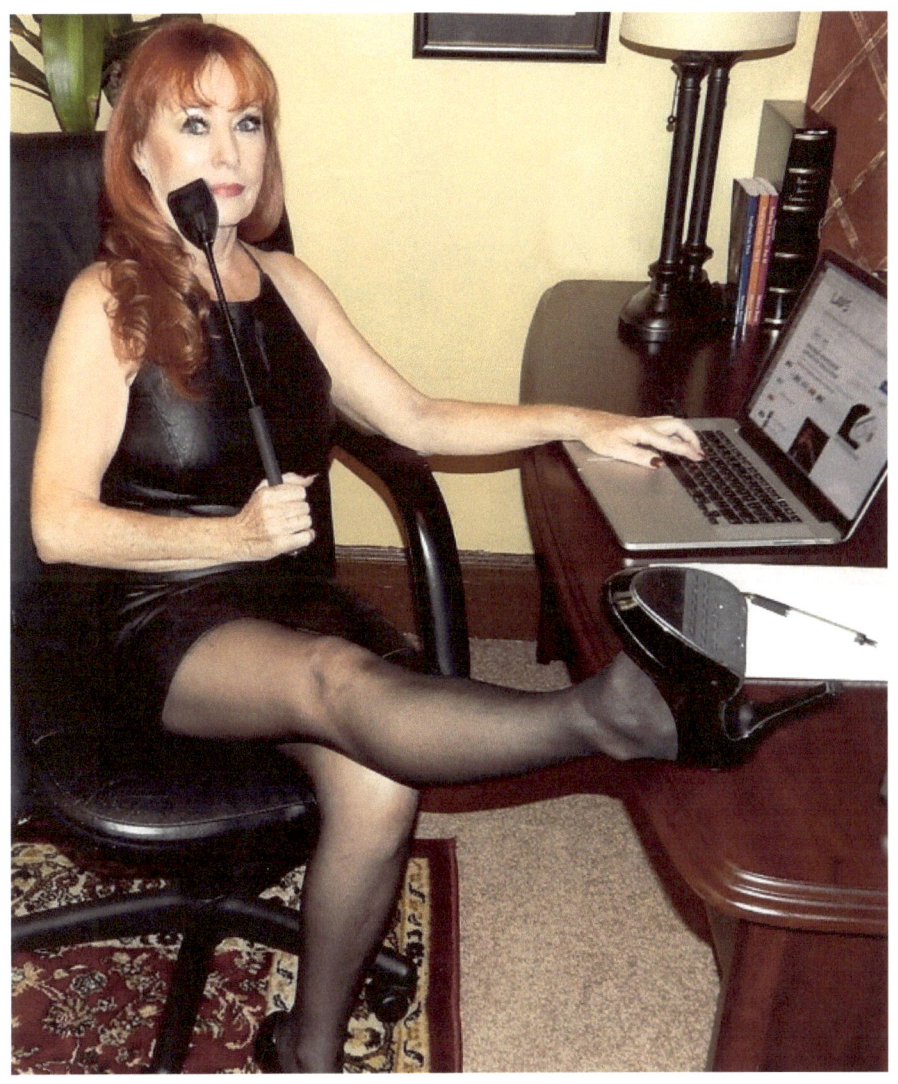

*Mistress Benay while She was working on her Top Selling
"FemDom Law Firm" Series*

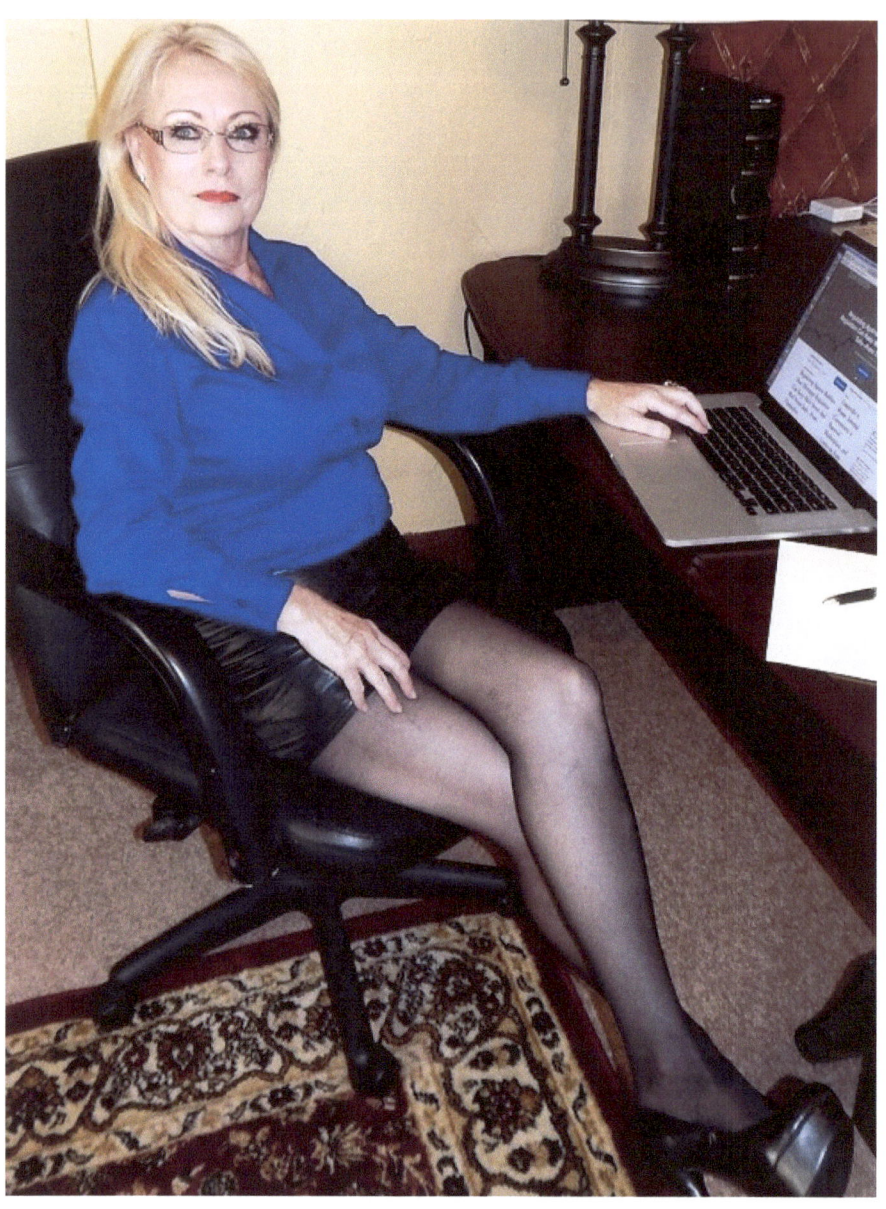

Mistress Benay working on her Award Winning Series
"His Fall From Power"

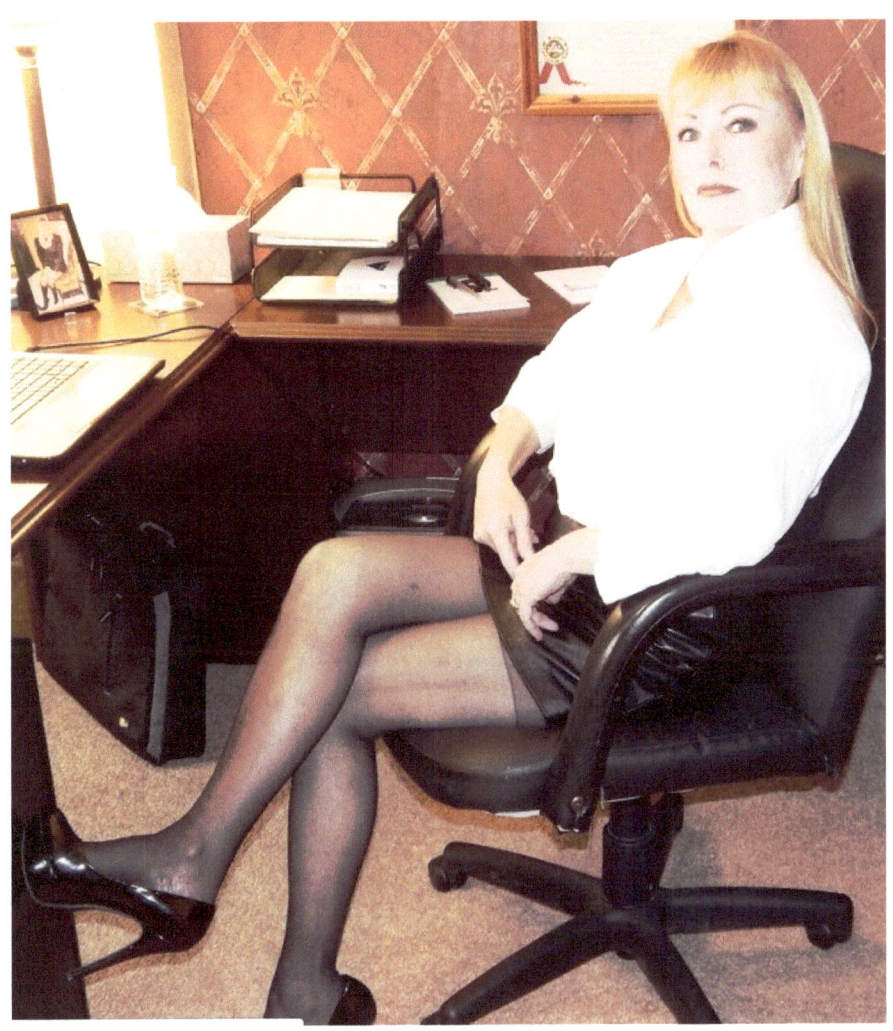

Behind The Scenes Photos of Mistress Benay

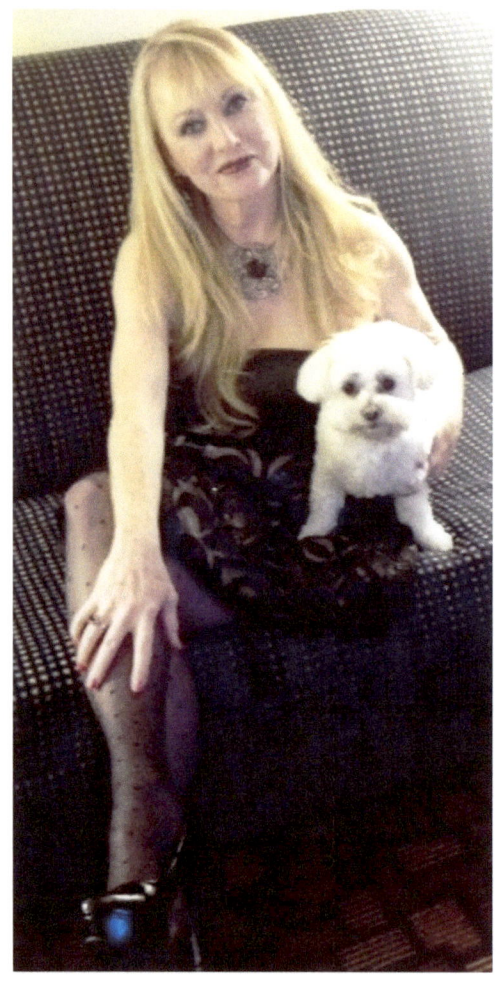

Mistress Benay with her Maltese - Bella Ragazza

Mistress Benay Getting Ready for a Photo Shoot

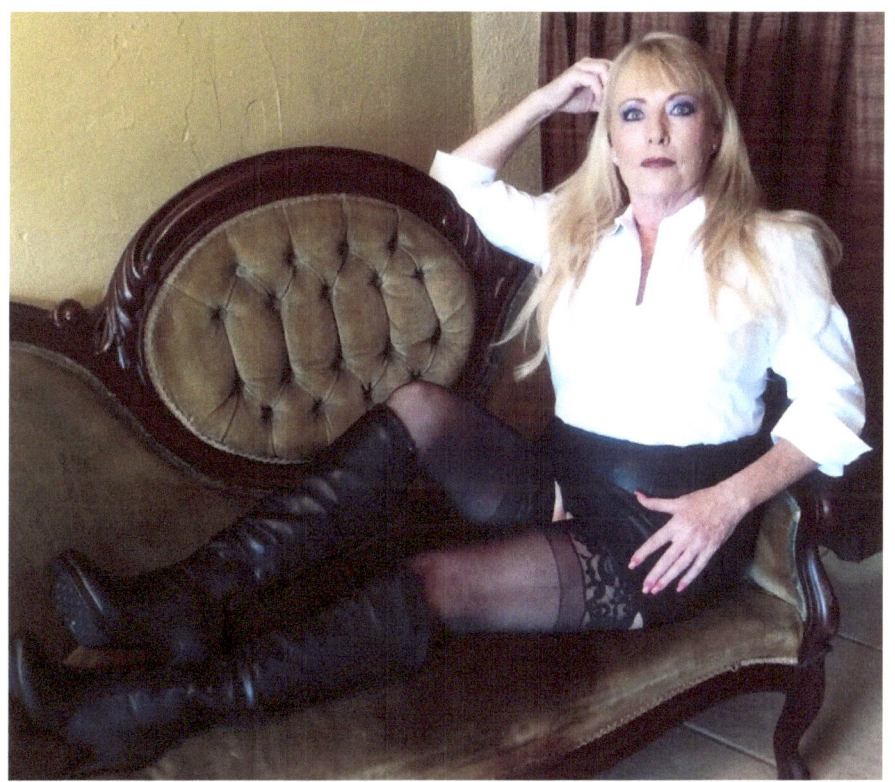

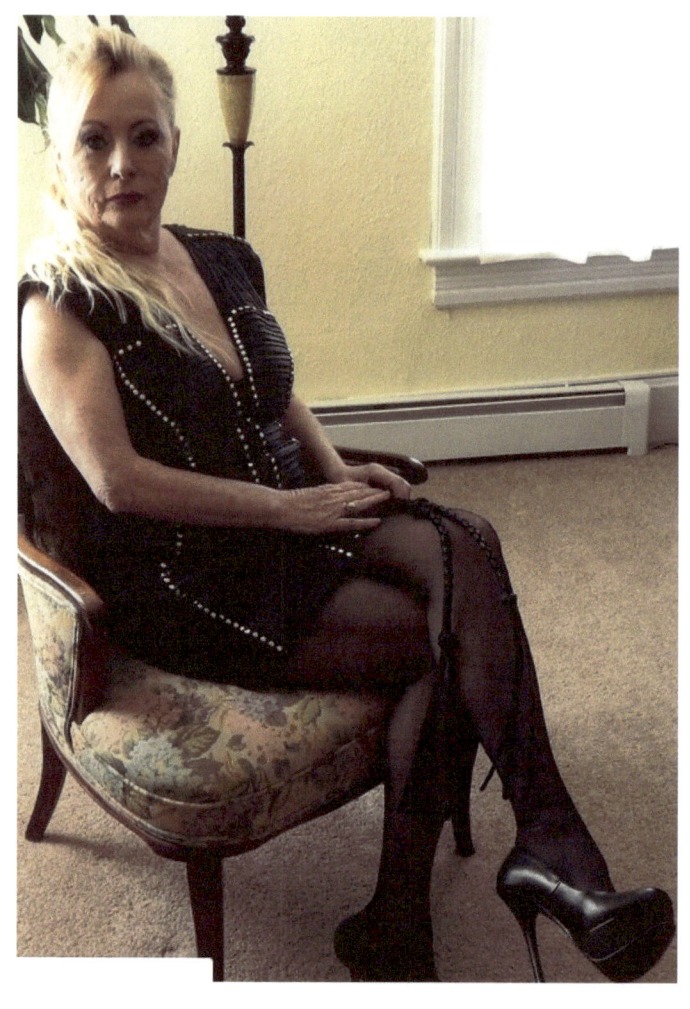

Photo Shoot for the Cover of "The Kinky Neighborhood"

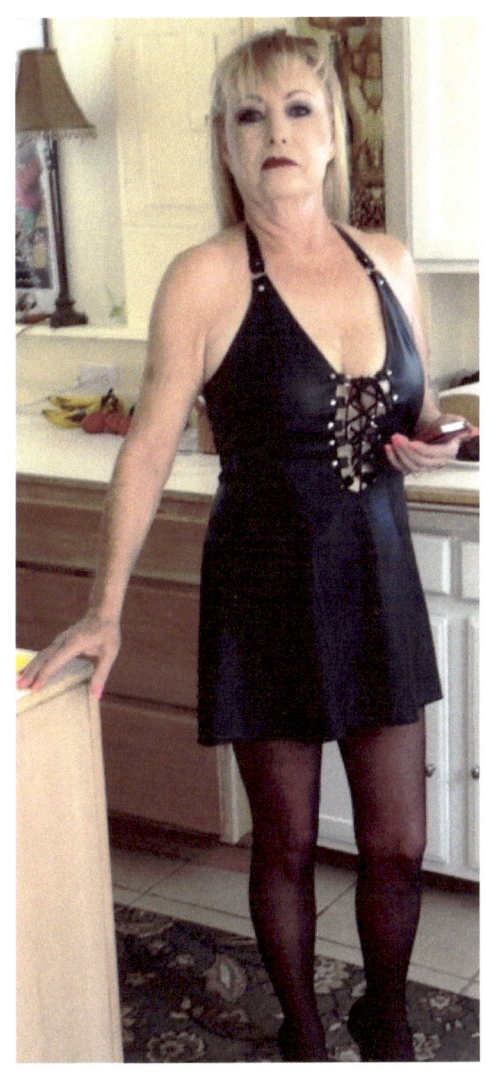

Taking a Break to catch up on Phone Calls during the Photo Shoot for "More Than He Ever Bargained For"

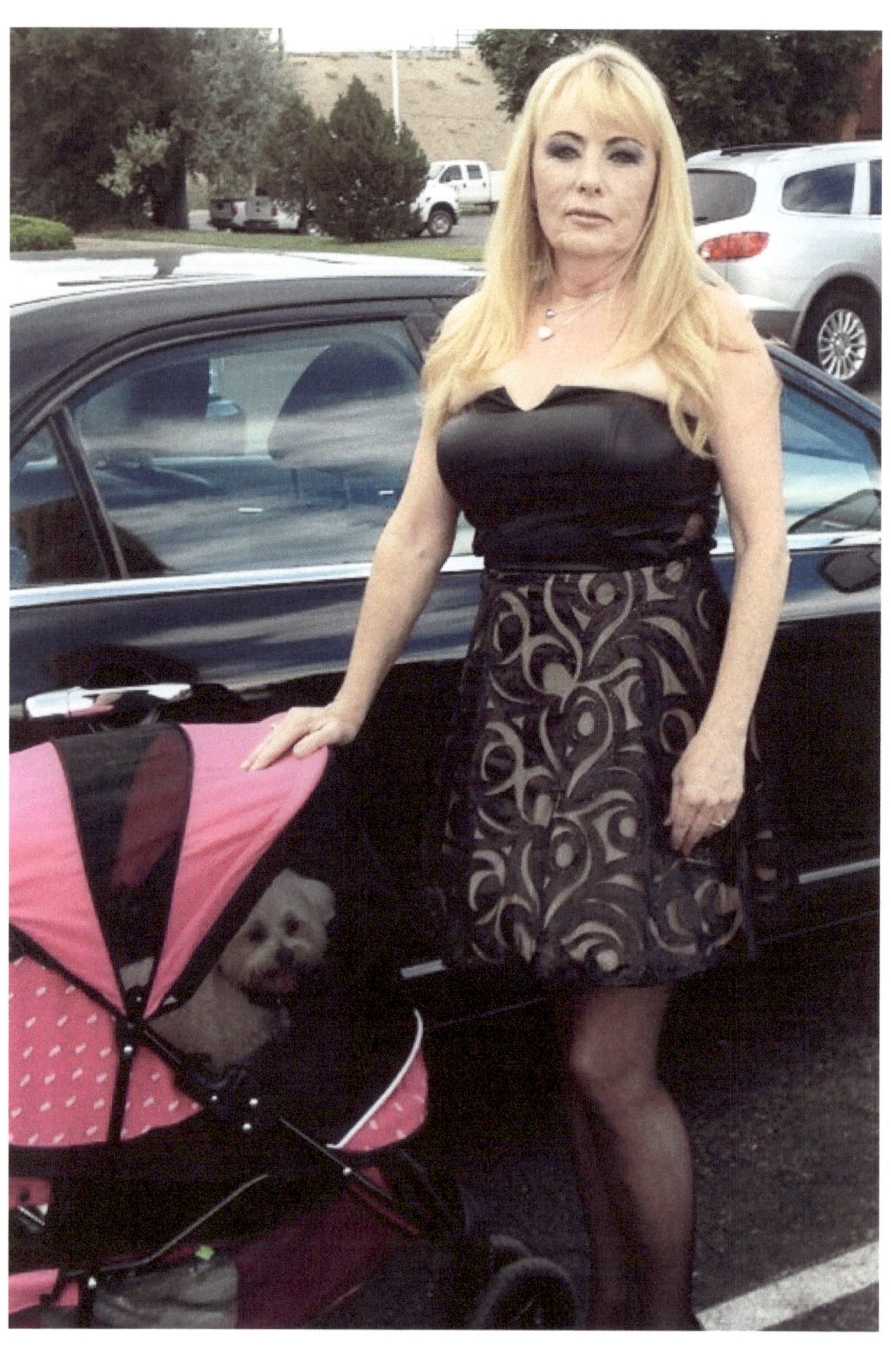

Dinner Break at Margarita's with Bella Ragazza

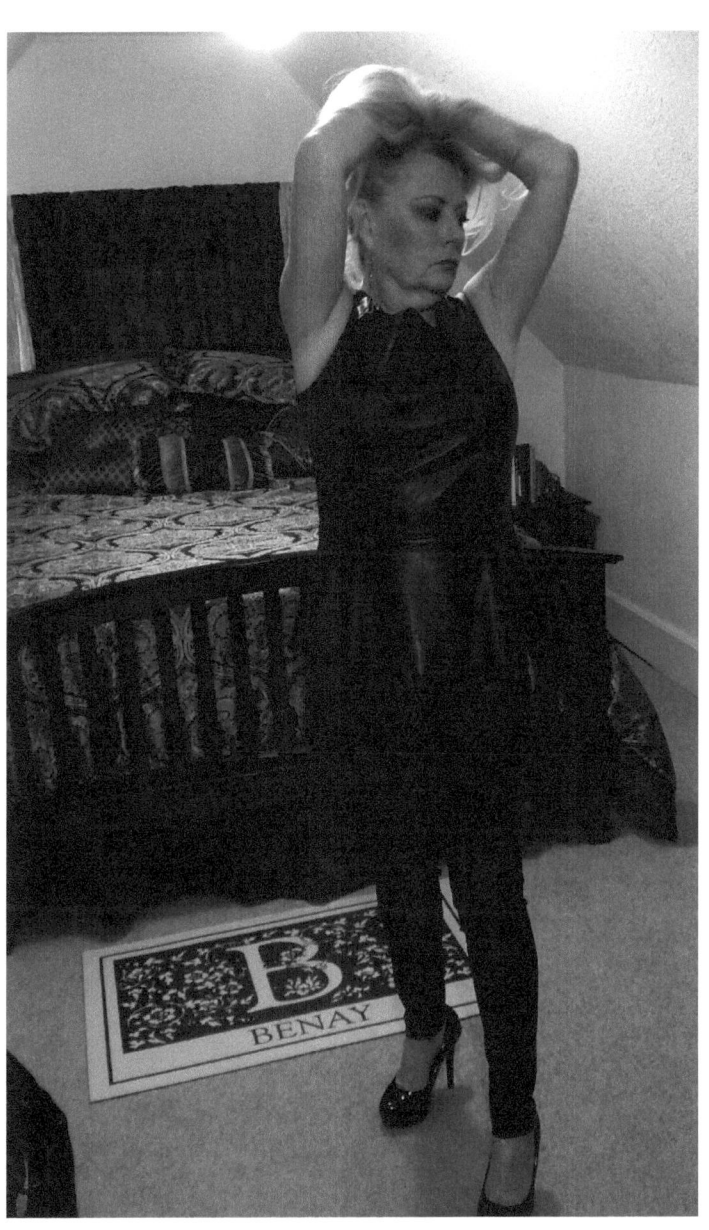

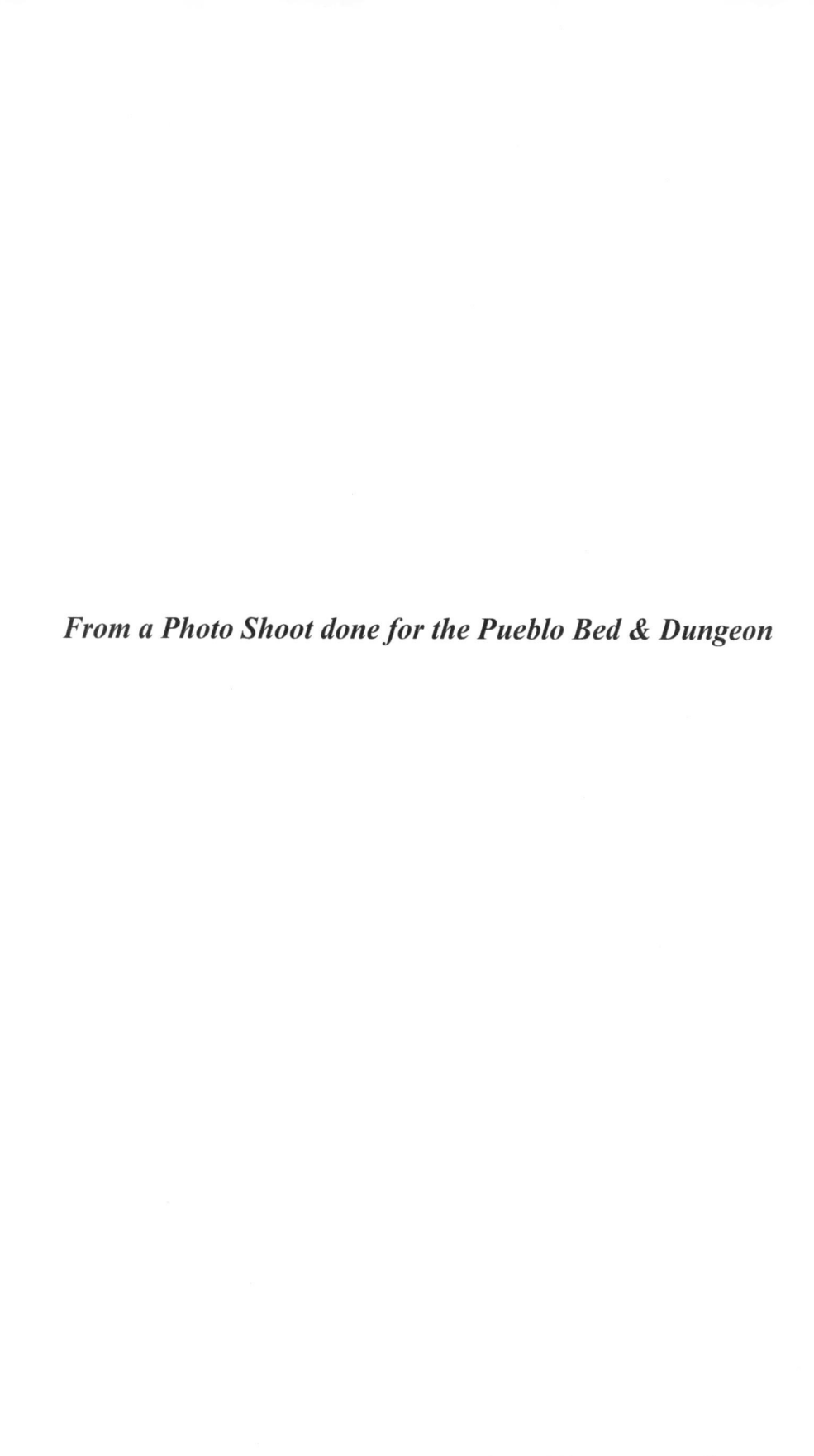

From a Photo Shoot done for the Pueblo Bed & Dungeon

One of Mistress Benay's Glamour Photos from the Pueblo Bed & Dungeon

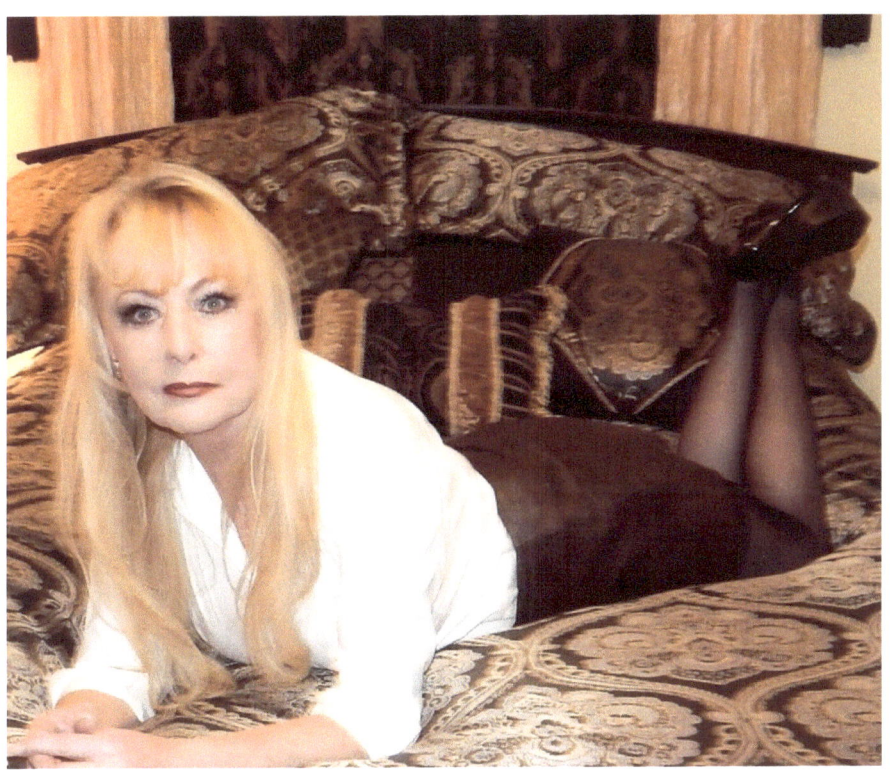

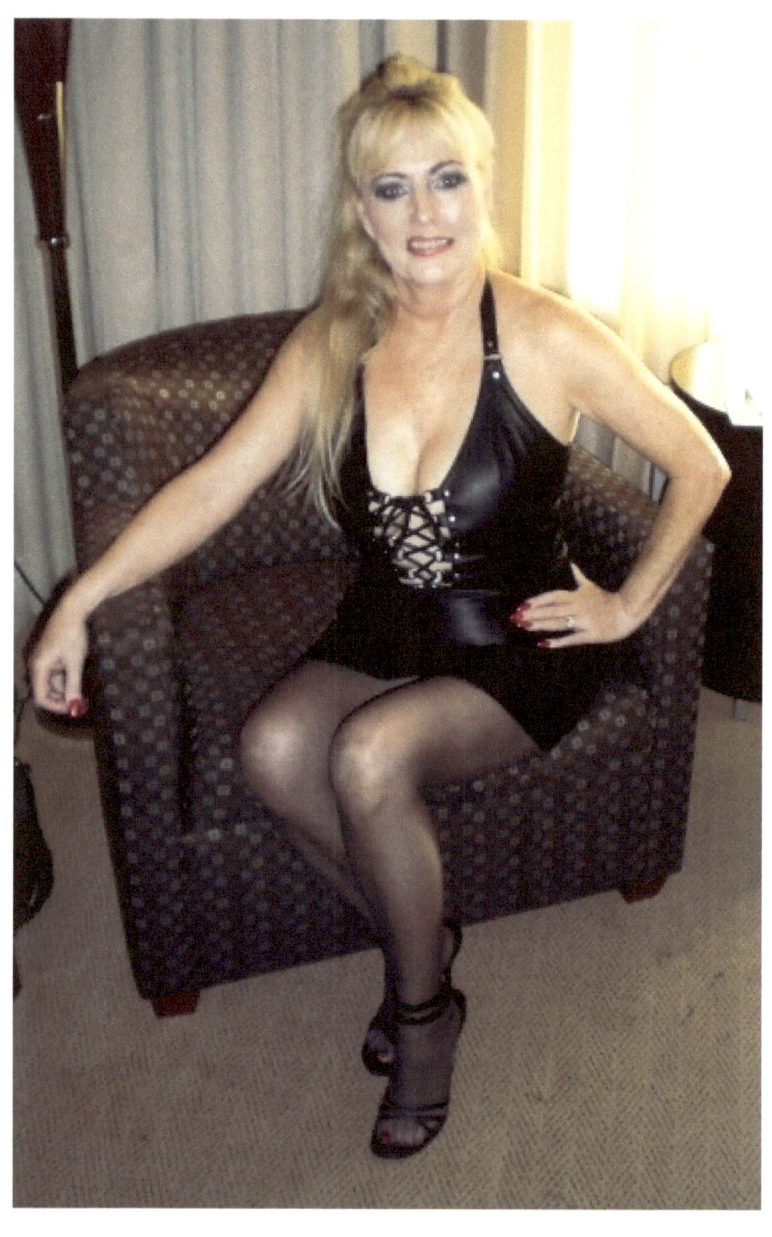

Photo Shoot for the Cover of "The Brother – In – Law"

Mistress Benay at Home & At Play - Enjoying Life

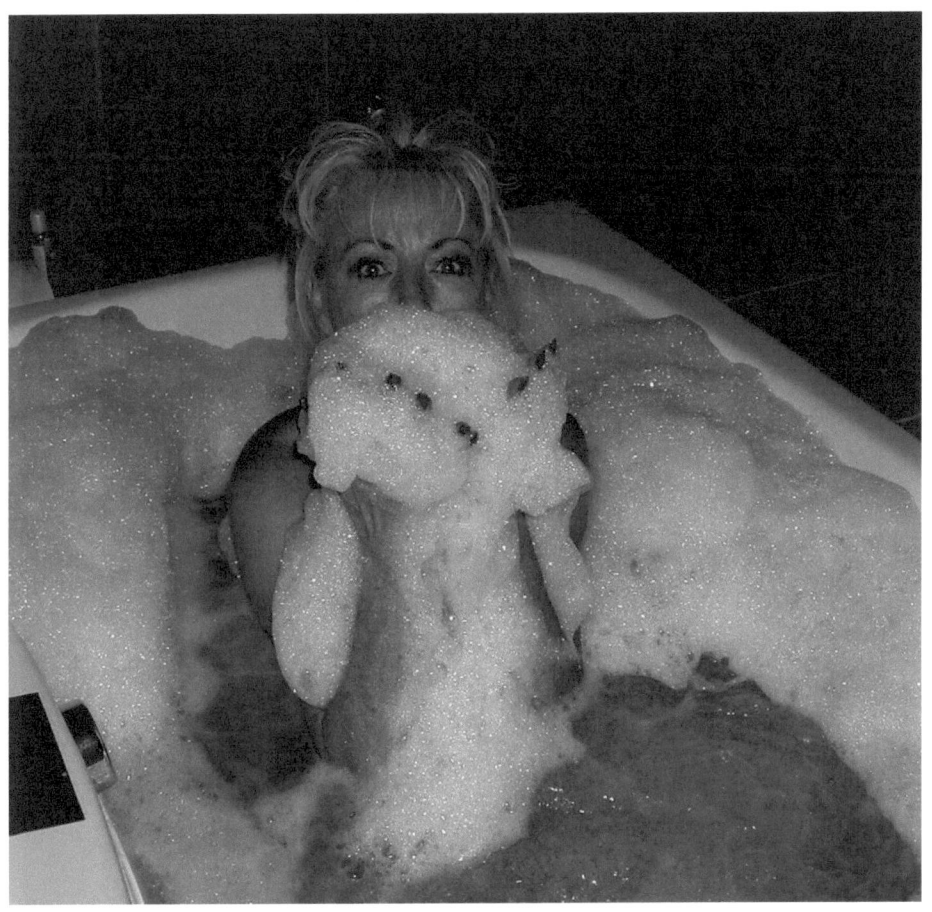

The Mistress's Cruise Ship makes a Stop In St. Thomas

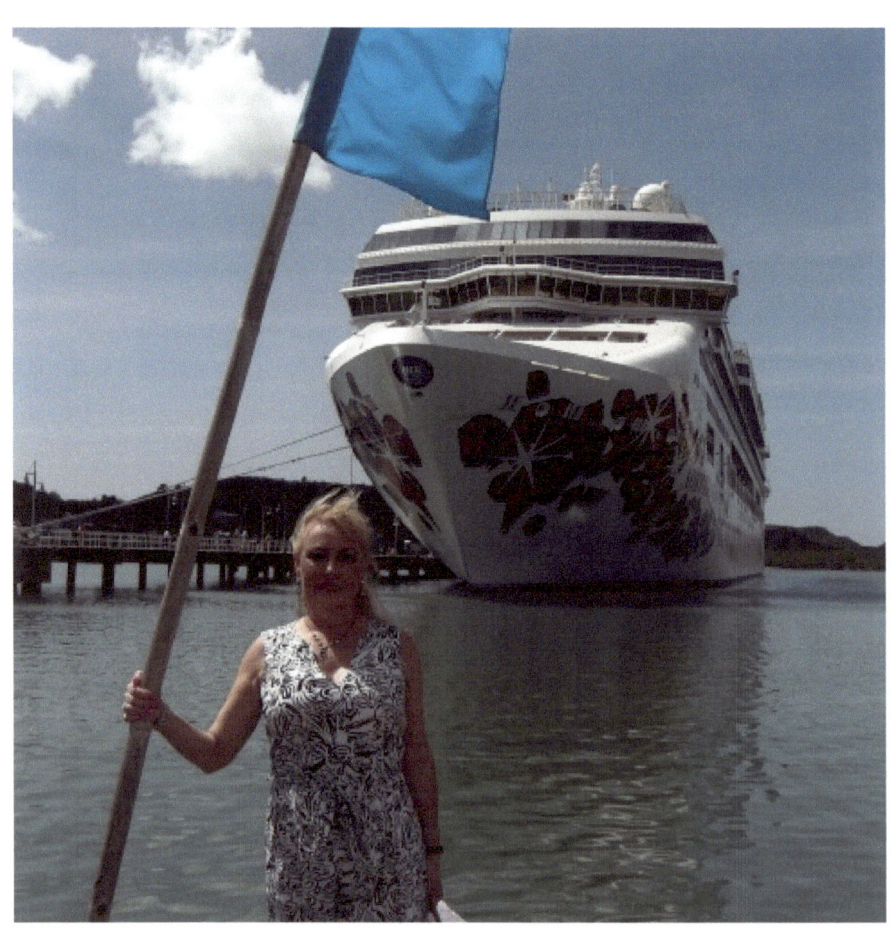

Smelling the Flowers on the Island of St. Thomas

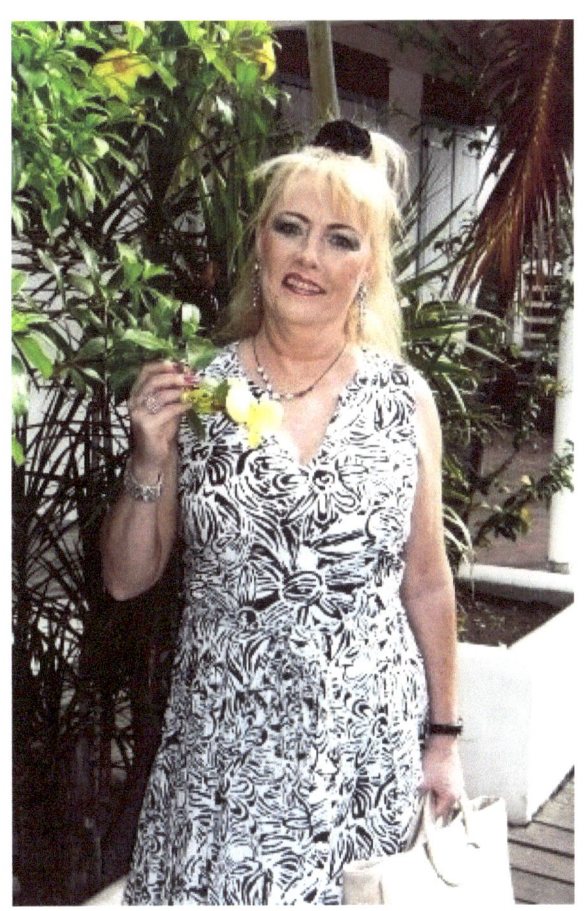

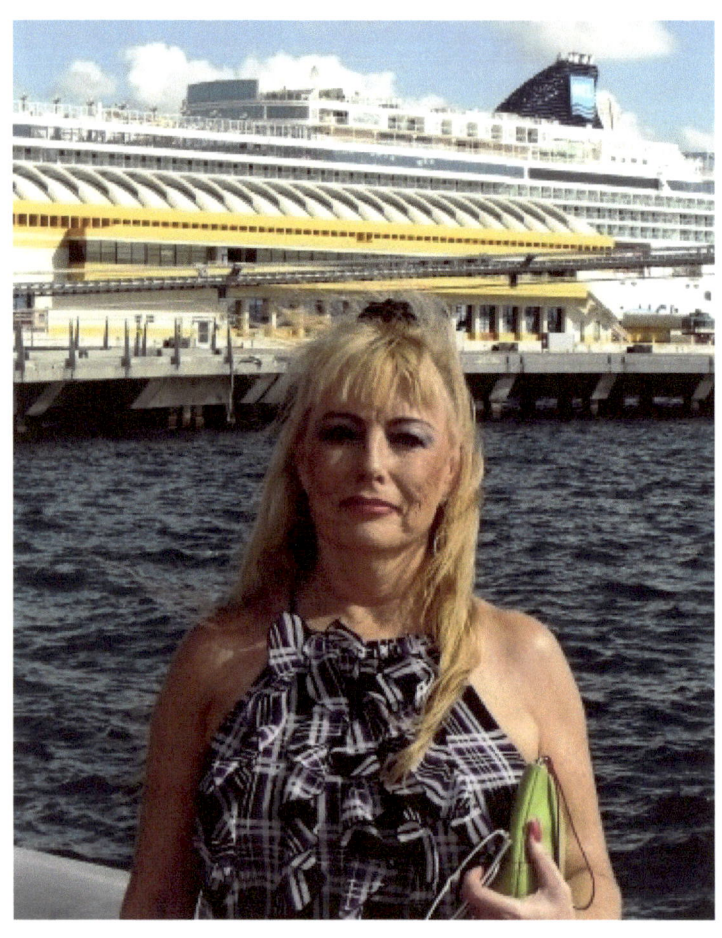

All Ready to Explore San Juan

Anniversary Dinner aboard the NCL Cruise Ship

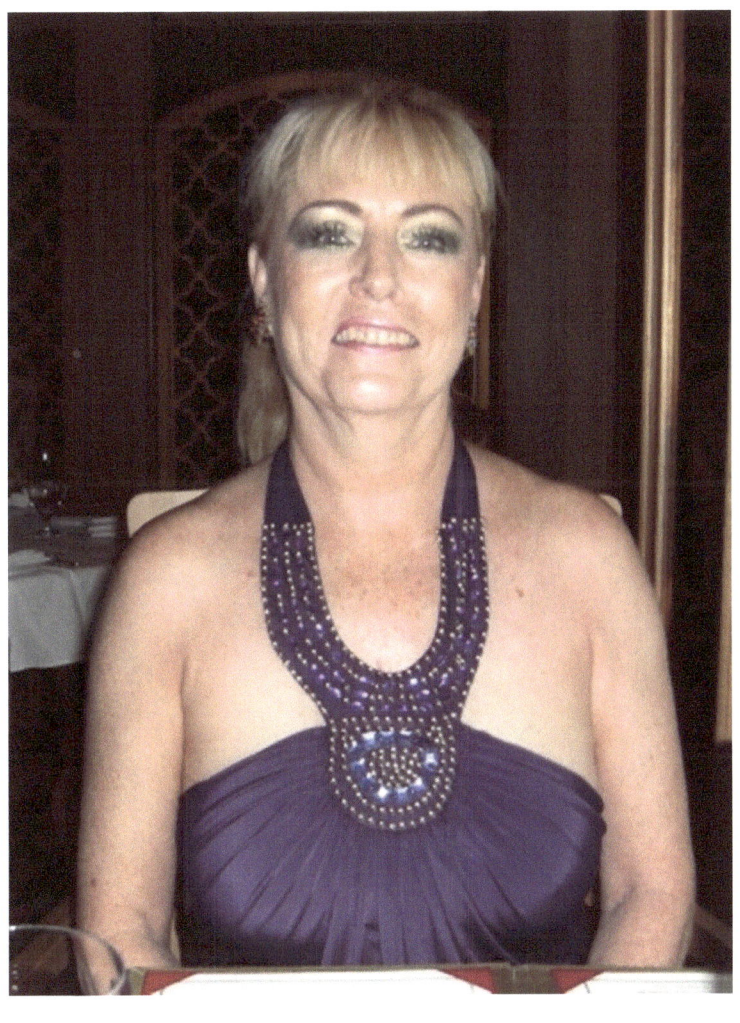

At the

Trump Taj Mahal in Atlantic City

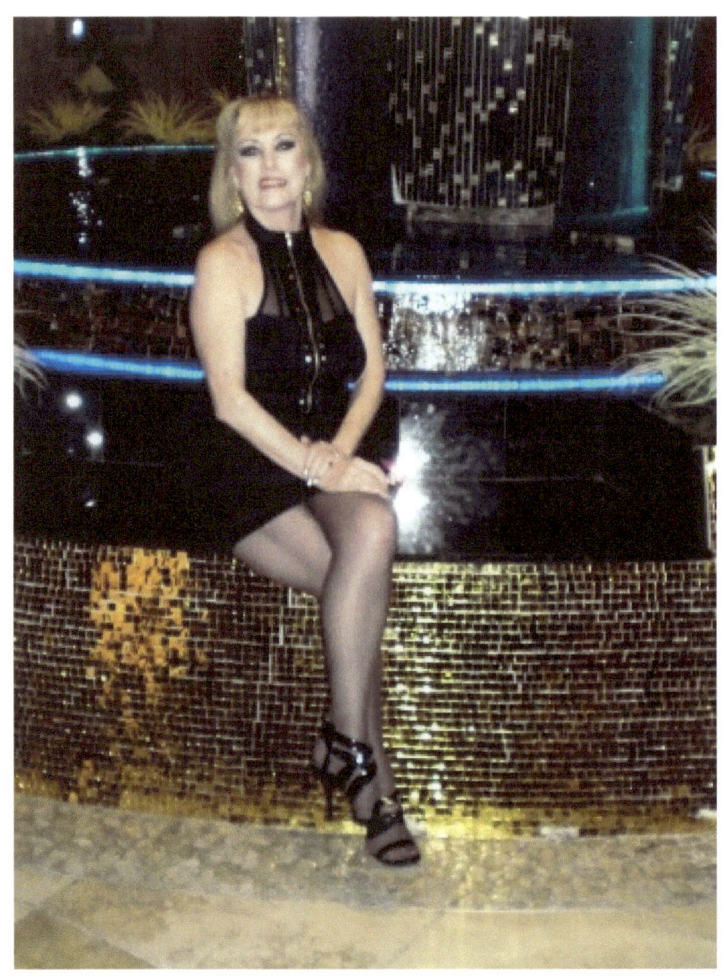

Exploring the Beach in Atlantic City

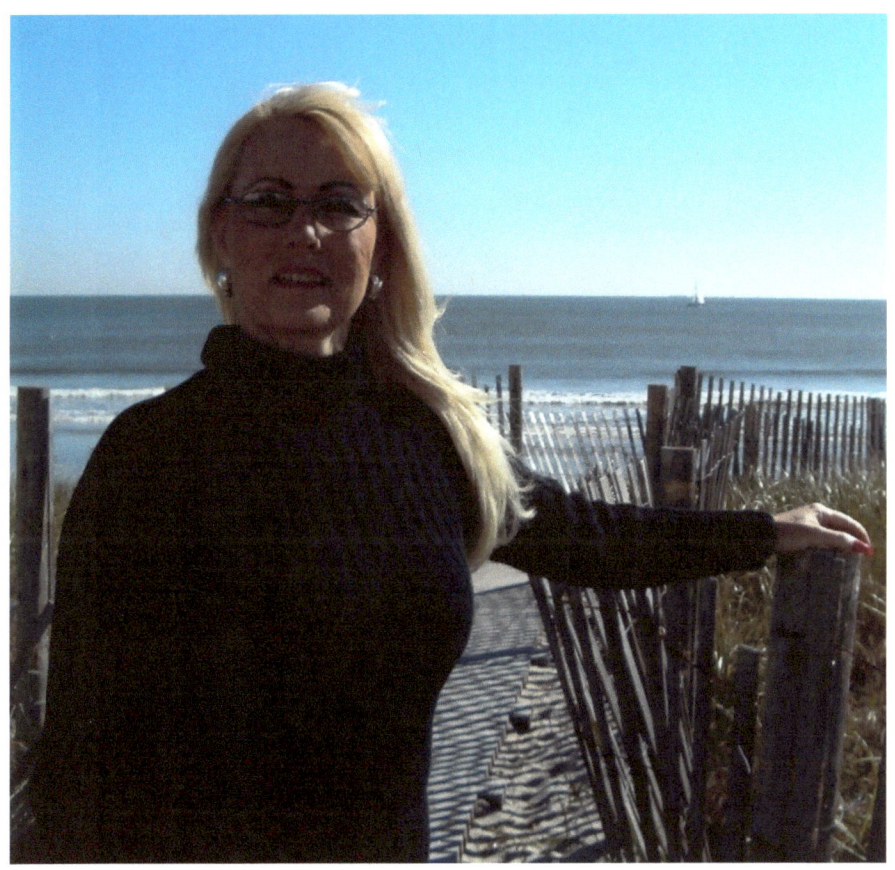

Looking for Treasures in the Shops of St. Thomas

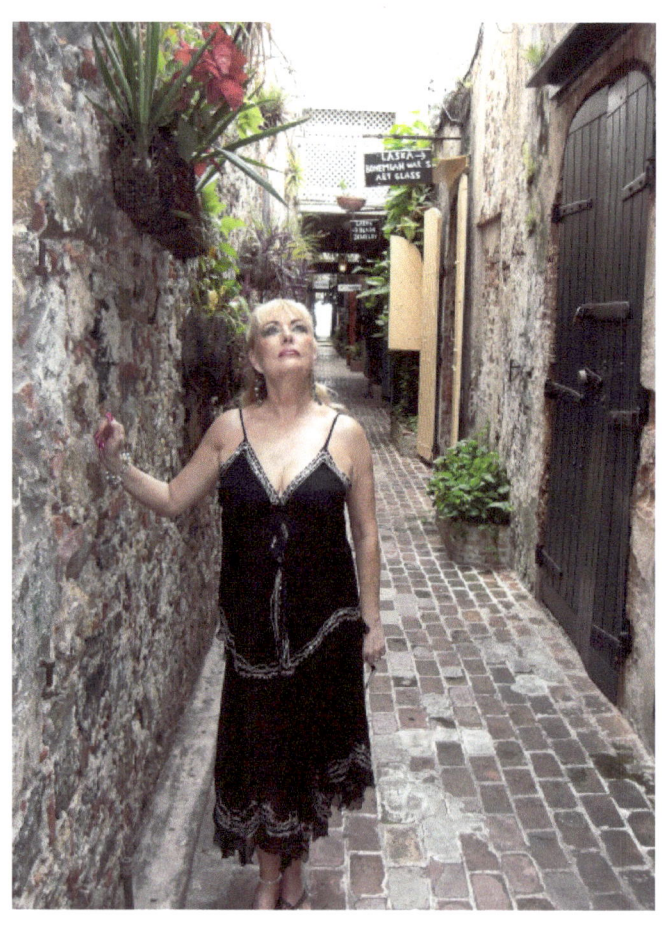

New Years Eve

Celebration with Frankie Valli and The Four Seasons at the Borgata in Atlantic City

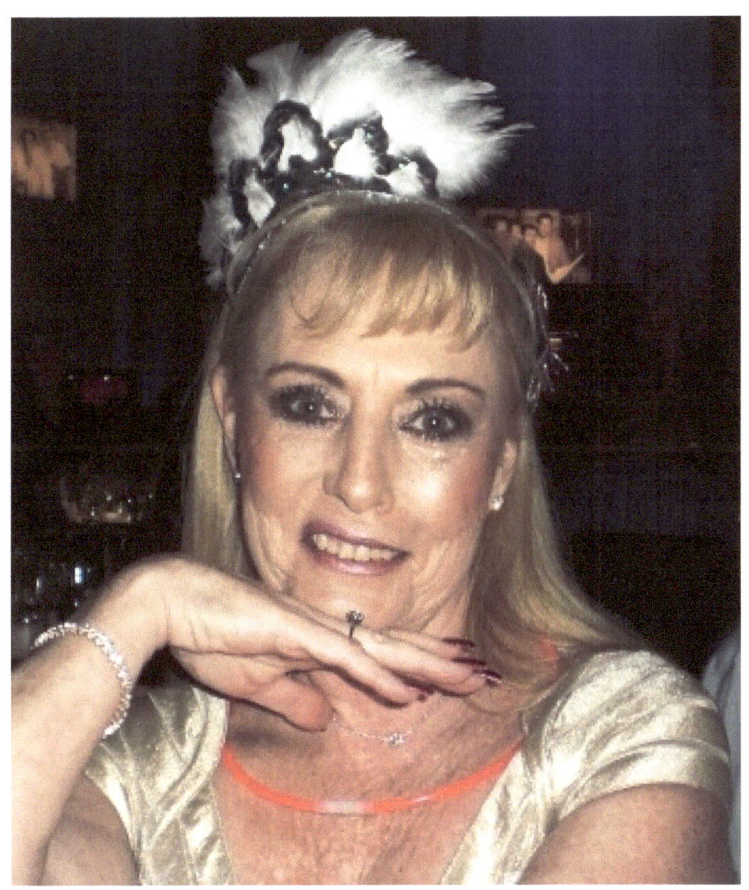

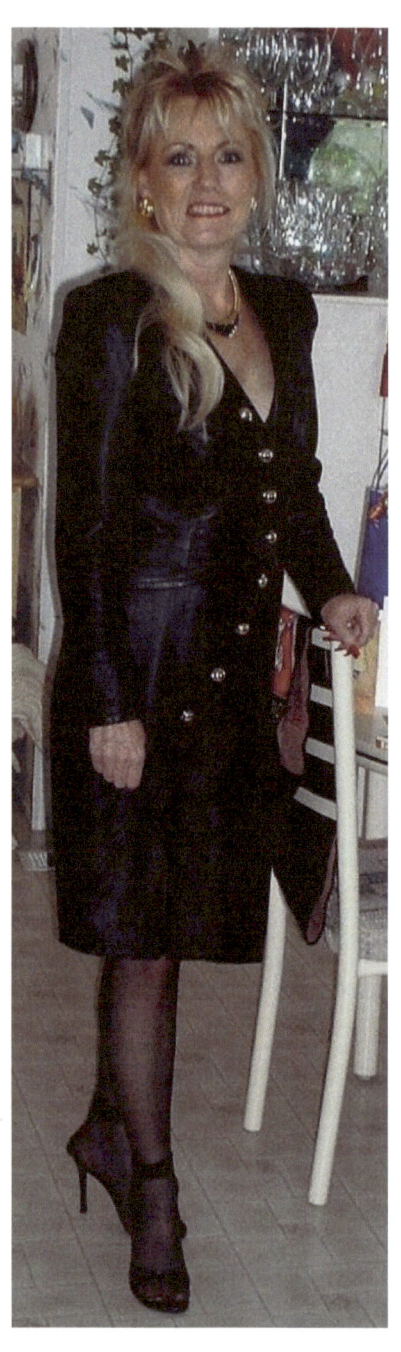

Mistress Benay getting ready for a Book Signing Event in Philadelphia

Weekend Get-A-Way at a Remote Cabin where Mistress Benay Locked Troy into a Chastity Cage for the First Time

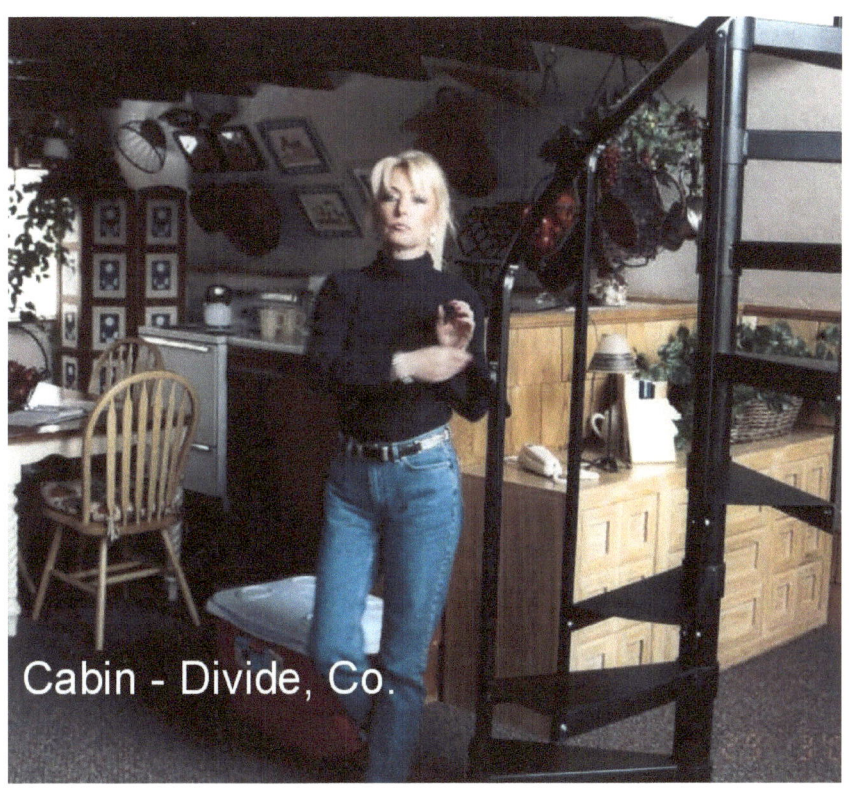

Cabin - Divide, Co.

A True Femme Fatale Visits Telluride, Colorado

(Definition of Femme Fatale: A Seductive Woman who lures men into Dangerous or Compromising Situations)

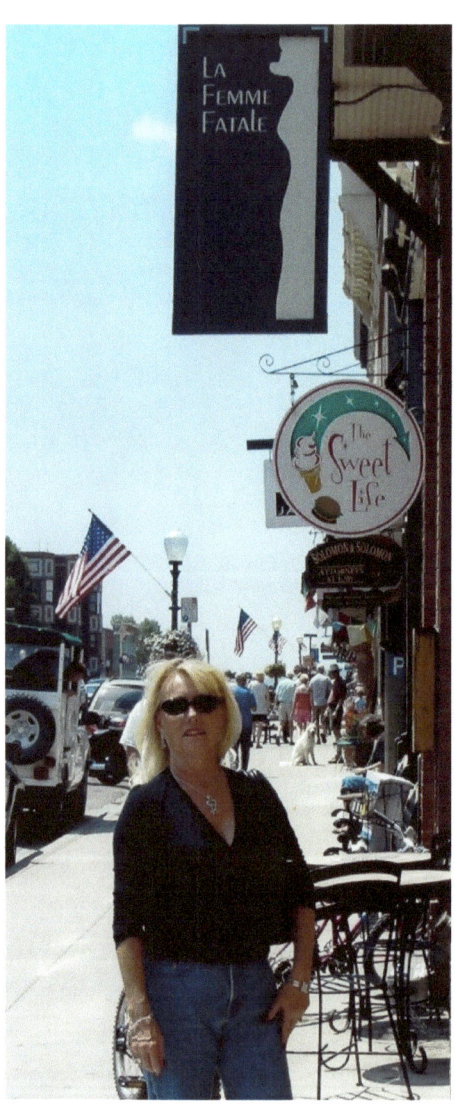

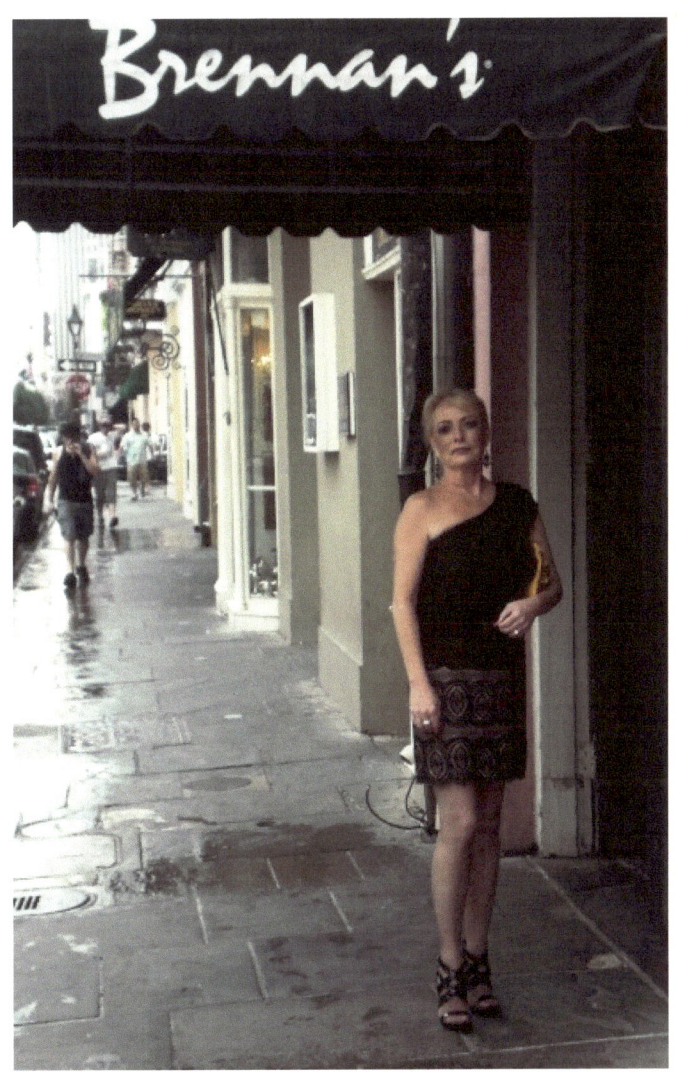

The Mistress getting ready to enjoy some Seafood in The Big Easy

Benay Sightseeing in New Orleans

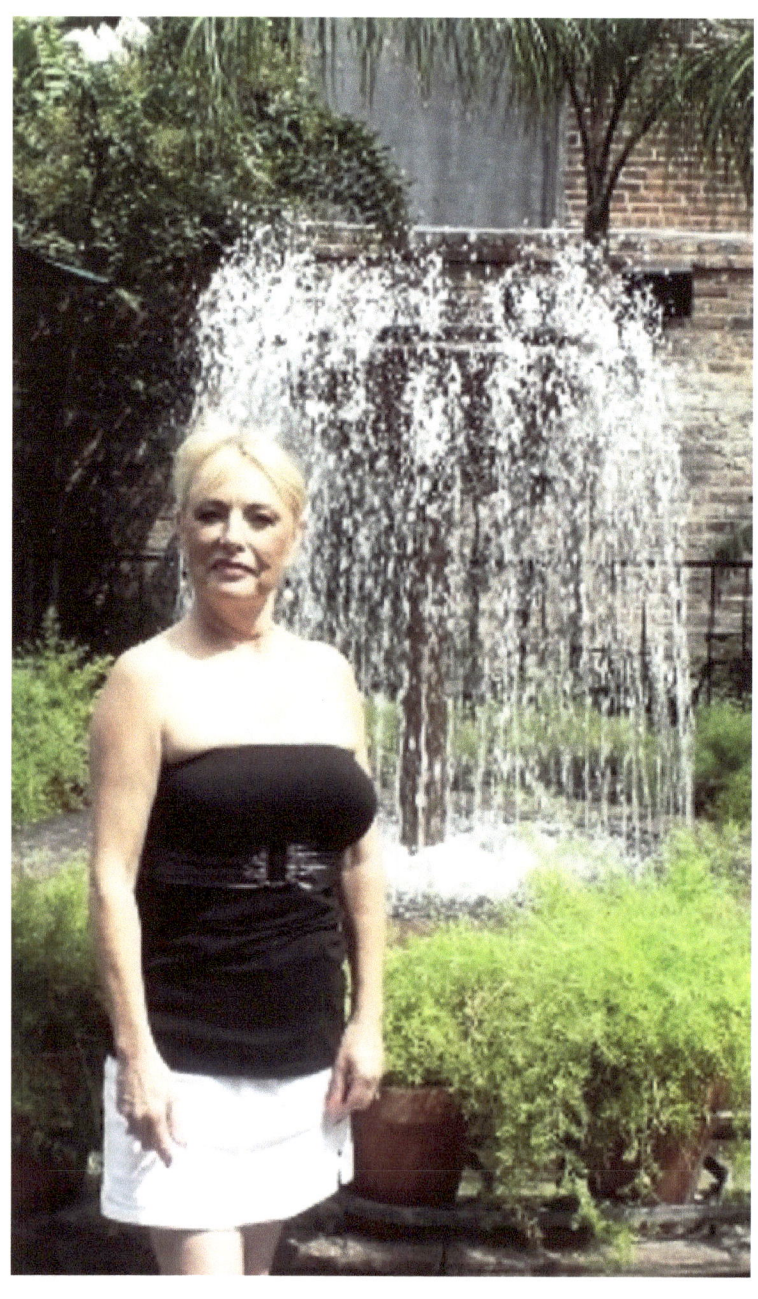

Benay Admiring her Favorite Painting Sunflowers by her Favorite Artist Van Gogh at the Philadelphia Art Museum

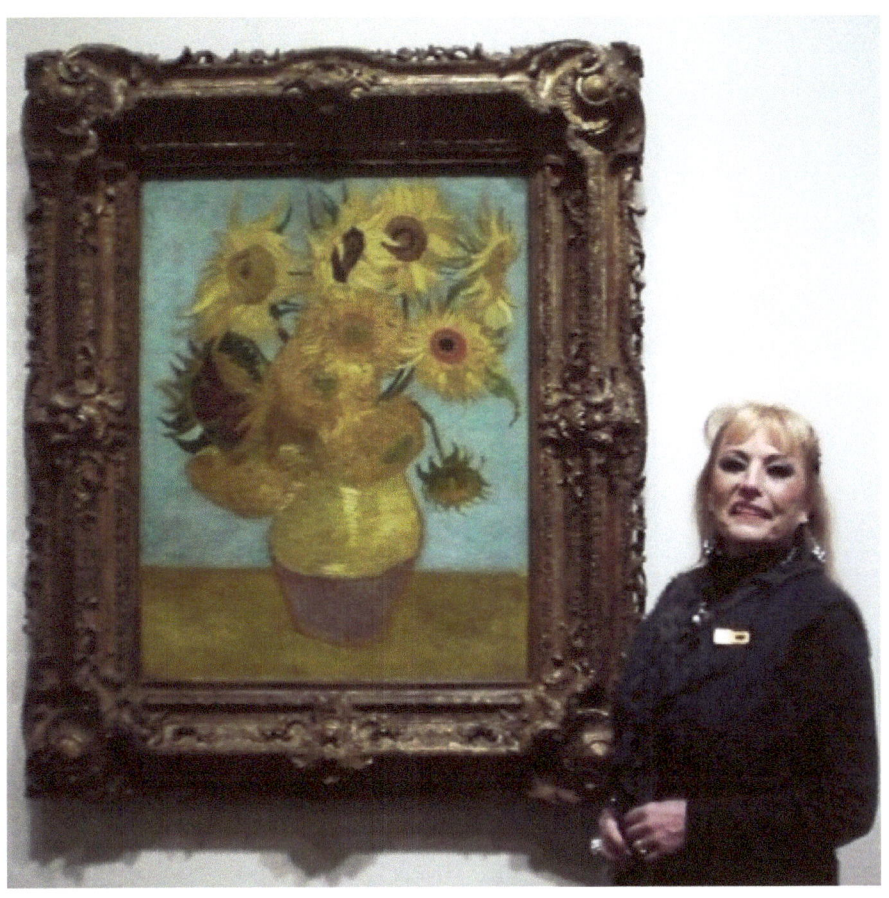

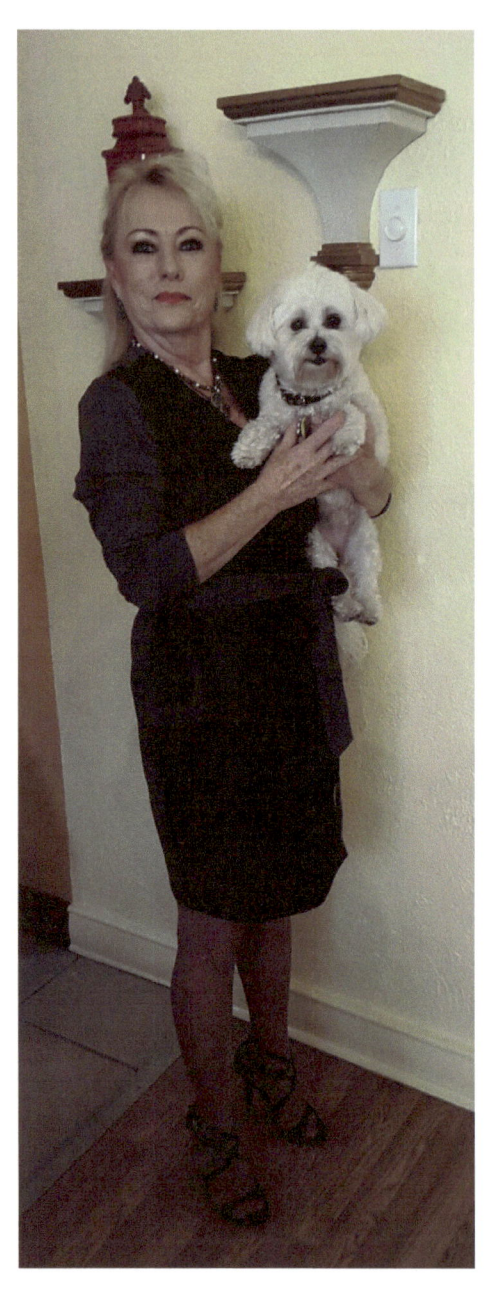

Benay spending Quality Time with her baby Bella Ragazza

Visiting the "Big Apple" to see the Rockettes and the Christmas Spectacular

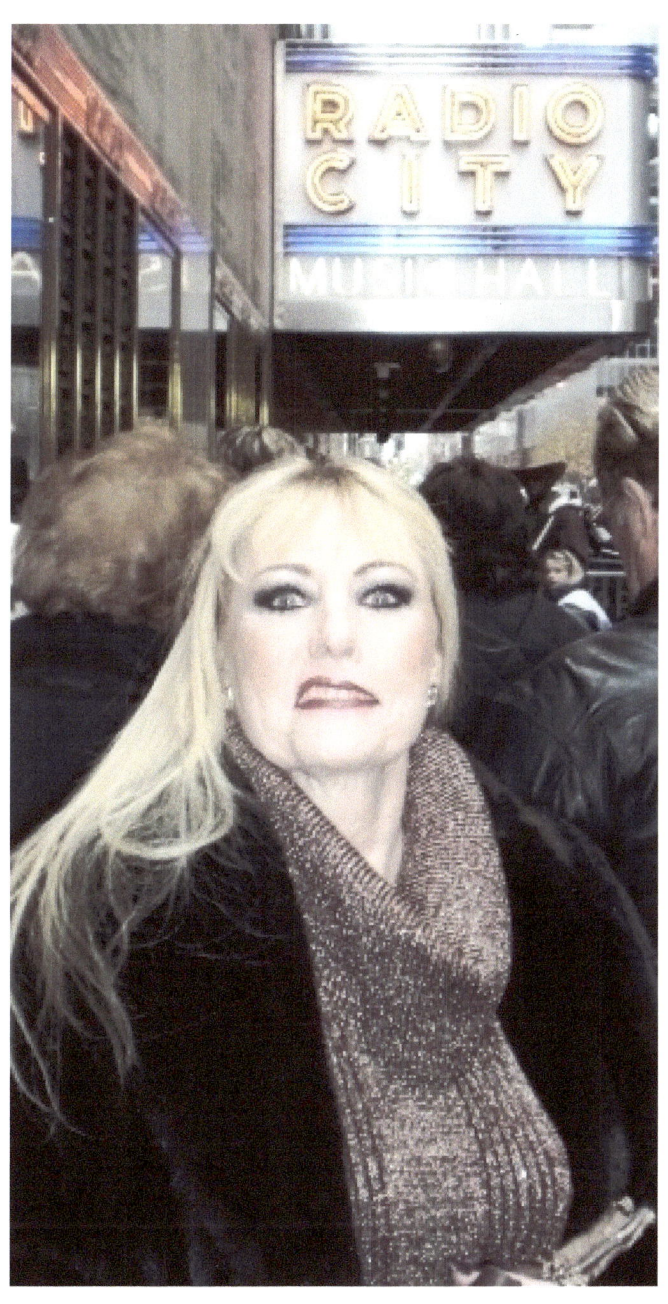

Waiting at the Colorado Springs Airport to Meet her slave's Incoming Flight

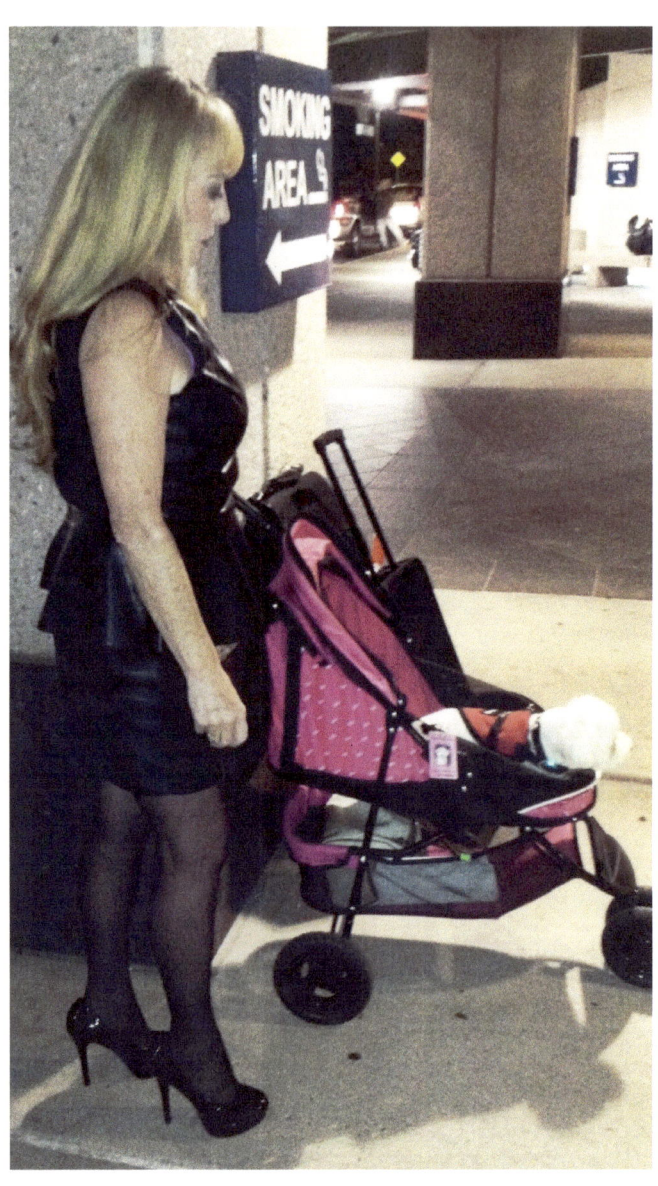

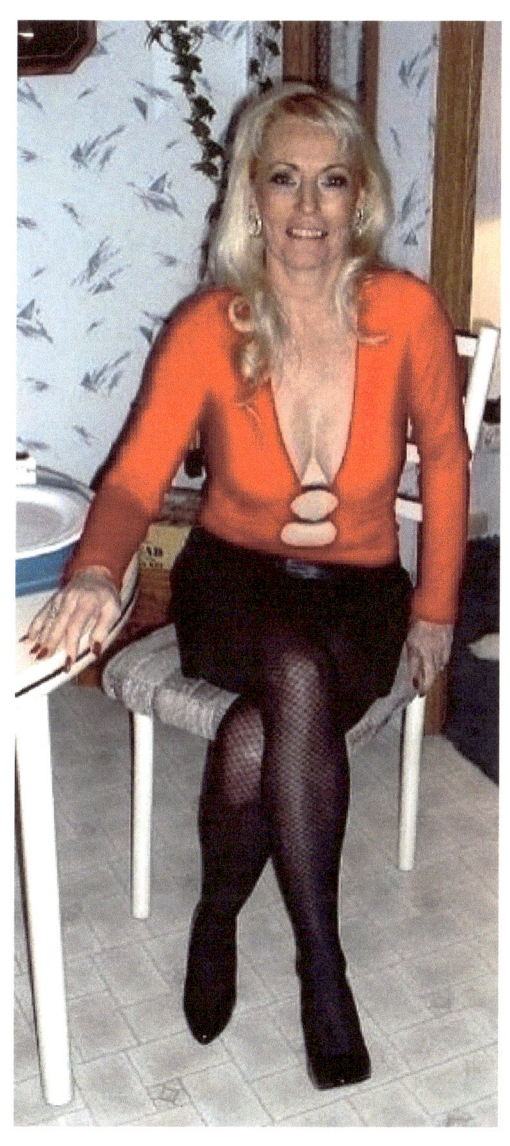

Mistress Benay – Always Elegant – Always Classy …
and Always So Positive and Full of Life.
You will Truly be missed by not only your Loving
Husband, but by Thousands of your Loyal Followers
and Readers!

We Will Never Forget You – We Will Always Love You!

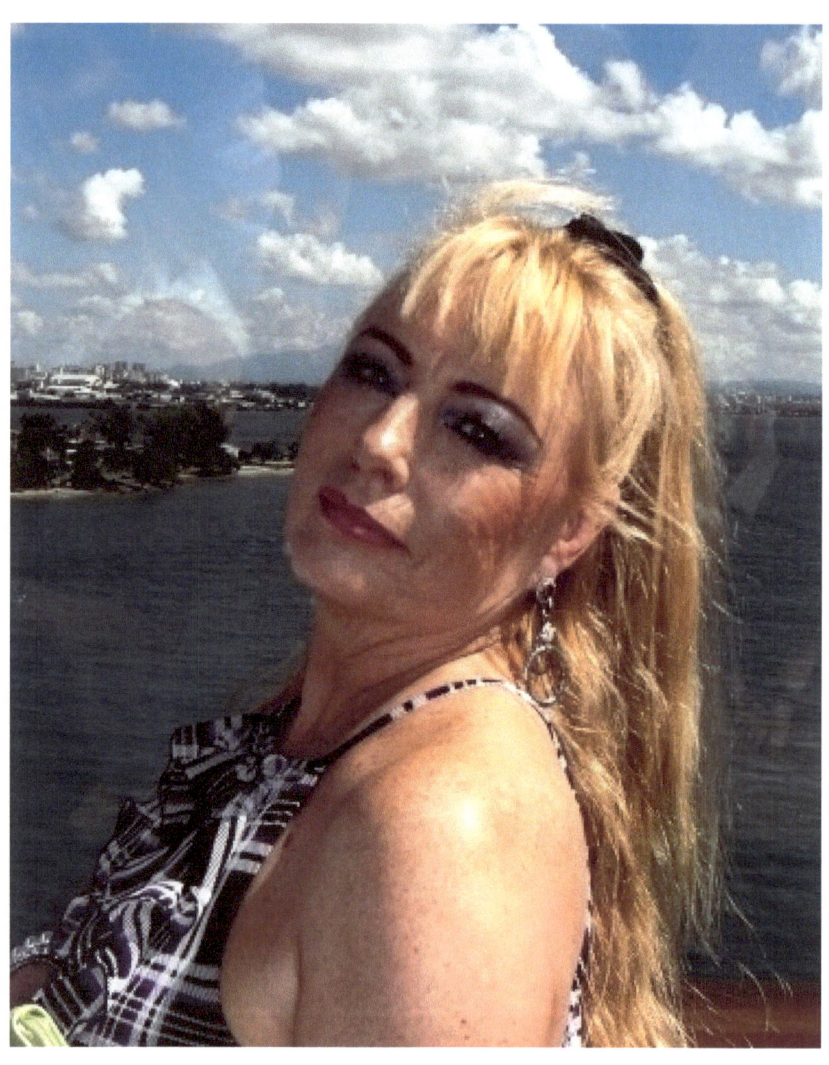

www.ingramcontent.com/pod-product-compliance
Lightning Source LLC
Chambersburg PA
CBHW041107180526
45172CB00001B/142